Introduction

THE Chinese short story developed to a high degree in the Tang dynasty (618-907), when excellently constructed tales with vivid characterization were written. These tales were known as *Chuan Qi* (Strange Stories), and were considered a lower form of literature than the classical essays of contemporary scholars. Before the Tang dynasty, China had already produced beautiful and moving stories and legends. Judging from extant works, some of these seem to have been inseparable from ancient fables — that is to say, legends were used to explain a philosophy — while others were used by Taoists, Buddhists and other religious sects to propagate their religion. Other tales recorded good deeds or sayings, clever repartee or jokes. The well-known *Shi Shuo Xin Yu* (New Anecdotes of Social Talk) is a good example of these. There were many collections of fairy tales, ghost stories and even travel accounts. All these pre-Tang stories were short and simply written — skeleton stories with little flesh on their bones. Not until the Tang dynasty do we find highly imaginative stories with detailed descriptions and realistic characterization.

One of the earliest Tang stories is *An Old Mirror*, written by Wang Du (c. 580-640) who lived at the end of the Sui and the beginning of the Tang dynasty. By combining several anecdotes about the magic power of old mirrors into one well-constructed story, Wang Du improved on the simple tales of the past.

The White Monkey, by an unknown writer of the middle of the seventh century, describes a monkey with magic powers, who carried off many beautiful women but was finally killed by a general. Although a story about the supernatural, it is filled with human feeling.

More important is *The Fairies' Cavern* by Zhang Zhuo (c. 660-740), a story of nearly ten thousand words. With a wealth of vivid detail, he describes how one night he entered a fairy cavern, and feasted and talked with the beautiful girls there. Zhang Zhuo's use of poetic imagery and folk sayings in this story had a great influence on later writers.

After this, stories of romantic love had a great vogue. Some were tragedies of real life, others were marvellous tales which had both sad and happy endings. *The Wandering Soul*, written by Chen Xuanyou toward the end of the eighth century, describes the love between Wang Zhou and Zhang Qianniang. When Qianniang's father ordered her to marry another man, Wang was heart-broken and indignant. He left by boat for the capital. But he could not sleep, and he was tossing about at midnight when he heard someone running along the bank — it was Qianniang who had come to join him. They went to Sichuan, lived together for five years, and had two sons. Then they decided to go back to Qianniang's old home. To their amazement, they found another Qianniang there lying ill in bed. All of a sudden the two girls' bodies merged in one, with one set of clothes over the other and it was clear that it was Qianniang's wandering soul which had run away with Wang.

Tang Dynasty Stories

Translated by
Yang Xianyi and Gladys Yang

Panda Books

Panda Books
First edition, 1986
Copyright 1986 by CHINESE LITERATURE
ISBN 0-8351-1602-6

With the exception of "The General's Daughter",
"The Jade Mortar and Pestle" and "The Prince's
Tomb", the present translations all appeared in
hardback in *The Dragon King's Daughter* (Foreign
Languages Press, Beijing, 1962).

Published by CHINESE LITERATURE, Beijing (37), China
Distributed by China International Book Trading Corporation
(GUOJI SHUDIAN) P.O. Box 399, Beijing, China
Printed in the People's Republic of China

CONTENTS

Ren the Fox Fairy, by Shen Jiji (c. 750-800), describes the love between a fox fairy and a young man named Zheng. It is a very vivid story. In the shape of a beautiful and charming girl, the fox shows herself loyal to her lover. Not even force can make her unfaithful to him. Later she is killed by a pack of hounds, but Zheng never forgets her.

The Dragon King's Daughter, written at the beginning of the ninth century by Li Chaowei, records the romance between a young man and the daughter of the dragon king of Dongting Lake. It is another story of the supernatural, full of human touches and with a well-constructed plot.

Even better than these, though, are *Prince Huo's Daughter* by Jiang Fang and *Story of a Singsong Girl* by Bai Xingjian, both of them based on real life. They give us a truthful and vivid picture of Tang society, while their pathos and power to keep us in suspense make them two of the finest examples of Tang stories.

Jiang Fang (c. 780-830) won fame as a poet early in his career, and held many high official posts. During the Chang Qing period (821-824), he was demoted to become Governor of Tingzhou. *Prince Huo's Daughter* describes the love between the famous poet Li Yi and a singsong girl called Huo Xiaoyu. He abandoned her to make a better match, and as she waited in vain for him to come back to her the girl fell ill. On her deathbed she saw Li Yi again and reproached him, then died of a broken heart. Readers cannot but share her indignation at the poet's heartlessness.

Bai Xingjian's *Story of a Singsong Girl* has a happy ending. The author was the younger brother of the famous poet Bai Juyi, and his works were popular with common folk. He wrote this story in AD 795 early in his career. The heroine of the story was a famous courtesan in the capital. The hero, Sheng, squandered all that he had for love of her, then became a beggar and suffered all kinds of hardships. Later the girl took him in again and encouraged him to study hard, so that finally he passed the civil service examination and became an official. This romantic story was extremely popular in its time.

The Story of Yingying by Yuan Zhen (779-831) exercised a great influence on later writers, and many poems and dramas were based on it, among them the famous opera *The Western Chamber*. Yuan Zhen was a poet who was almost as popular as his contemporary Bai Juyi. His poems were widely read and known even in the imperial palace, where he was considered a genius. He held important official posts, and has left over a hundred works. He was the best known of Tang short story writers. *The Story of Yingying* is a love story which ends in tragedy, since both the hero and heroine are forced to marry others. (The opera *The Western Chamber* substitutes a happy ending for this.) But the description of first love in this work is unforgettable.

The well-known *Song of Everlasting Sorrow* was written by Chen Hong, a friend of Bai Juyi who had written a poem with this title to describe the love of Emperor Ming of the Tang dynasty for the Lady Yang. Chen Hong wrote this story to be appended to the poem. It had a great influence on later writers, although it is simply written and not particularly moving.

There were a great number of love stories of this nature in the Tang dynasty, but most of them were of the types mentioned above.

Tang readers also enjoyed highly imaginative escap-
ist stories which showed how wealth and fame could
vanish like a dream. The incidents in these dream tales,
however, were thoroughly realistic. Such stories show
the discontent and aspirations of scholars under the
Tang examination system, for while they satirize the
pomp and splendour of high officials and show how
often they came to a sad end, readers can detect an
undercurrent of envy on the part of writers who had
failed in their career. Examples of such stories are *The
Story of the Pillow* by Shen Jiji, *Dream of Qin* by Shen
Yazhi and *Governor of the Southern Tributary State* by
Li Gongzuo — the last of these stories being the best.

Li Gongzuo was a good friend of Bai Xingjian, and
they both wrote excellent stories. Like Bai's *Story of a
Singsong Girl*, Li's *Governor of the Southern Tributary
State* was not only famous in its day, but also exercised
a great influence on later writers, especially later
dramatists. These two stories are totally different in
atmosphere though. Li Gongzuo as a low-ranking official
must have had a hard life, and in his story we sense a
passive protest, for he resorts to escapism to disguise
his discontent and unhappiness. The life of Chunyu
Fen in the ant heap is the life of the greatest Tang officials, and this story is a true expression of the psycho-
logy of Tang bureaucrats. *The Story of the Pillow* and
Dream of Qin have similar themes. Shen Yazhi
(c. 790-850) was a friend of the poet Li He, who thought
him a genius. He too was a petty official, whose works
are still extant; but his *Dream of Qin* is much inferior
to *Governor of the Southern Tributary State*.

In AD 755 An Lushan revolted, and the central power
of the Tang empire began to decline, while local war-

lords grew stronger and controlled larger and larger areas. In order to consolidate their political power and extend their territory, these warlords exploited and enslaved the people cruelly. The common folk led a wretched life. In addition to paying heavy taxes, they had to serve as soldiers for the warlords who wanted to seize more land. The situation became more serious after the reign of Emperor Xuan Zong (806-821) until it led to the great rebellion headed by Huang Chao in AD 875. The warlords of this period kept knights and assassins, while the suffering people hoped that superhuman champions would come forward to right their wrongs and overthrow the tyrants. This accounts for the popularity of stories about superhuman champions or swordsmen.

The Man with the Curly Beard by Du Guangting belongs to this genre, differing from other stories of this type only in its loyalty to the Tang dynasty — Du Guangting maintains that the Tang emperors ruled by divine right and must not be overthrown. But the mysterious man with the curly beard in this story is one of the swordsmen of the time. Du Guangting, who lived at the beginning of the tenth century, was a Taoist priest. He went to Sichuan during a period of civil strife, and was made a minister by the local ruler. His stories are still read today, and the theme of *The Man with the Curly Beard* was borrowed by later dramatists.

Stories and Anecdotes of You Yang by Duan Chengshi (800?-863) contains many tales about gallants. *Red Thread*, from the anecdotes of Yuan Jiao written in the middle of the ninth century, is another good story of this type. Red Thread was a remarkably gifted girl who could travel very swiftly, and thanks to her skill

as a swordswoman she succeeded in stopping a war between two rival generals. This story later enjoyed great
popularity. The stories of Pei Xing, written about the
same time, are mostly of this type too, the best known
being *The General's Daughter* and *The Kunlun Slave*.
The Kunlun Slave is simply the story of a brave man,
while *The General's Daughter* contains a supernatural
element. The story of the general's daughter, a girl
famed for her miraculous swordsmanship, was the fore-
runner of many tales of a similar type. Pei Xing served
as secretary to Gao Bin, military governor of Qinghai
during the Xian Tong period (860-873), and was later
promoted to the post of vice governor of Chengdu
and the position of Knight Adviser. Gao Bin was fond
of the supernatural, and Pei Xing might have come
under his influence in this respect. But although he
wrote about supernatural beings and swordsmen, his
stories give us a picture of the real social conditions of
those troubled times.

Tang stories are obviously a great advance upon the
simple stories and legends of earlier dynasties. They
give delicate and detailed descriptions of both real and
imaginary situations. A Song dynasty critic wrote: "We
should study the Tang stories. Slight as they are, they
possess exquisite pathos, and stand with Tang poetry as
one of the glories of their age." This is a fair criticism.
These stories exercised a great influence on later Chinese writers. Many story-tellers imitated their style, and
they were a source of material for dramatists. Many
operas of the Yuan and the Ming dynasties, like *The
Western Chamber, Governor of the Southern Tributary
State* and *The Embroidered Coat*, borrowed the themes
of Tang stories. Thus their position in the history of

Chinese literature may be compared to that of the myths and legends of Greece. Chinese writers and artists cannot dispense with a good knowledge of these stories, and students of Chinese literature have to study them too, for it is impossible otherwise to understand the origin and development of the themes of many later works.

But these stories are worth reading for their own sake. Not only is their content enchanting, but they have achieved a high degree of artistic excellence.

Zheng Zhenduo

Ren the Fox Fairy

Shen Jiji

WEI Yin, ninth son of the daughter of the Prince of
Xinan, was a somewhat wild young lord and a heavy
drinker. His cousin's husband, Zheng, whose personal
name is not known but who was the sixth child of his
family, had studied the military arts and was also fond
of drinking and women. Since he was poor and had
no home of his own, he lived with his wife's family.
Zheng and Wei became inseparable. In the sixth month
of the ninth year of the Tian Bao period (AD 750), they
were walking together through the capital on their way
to a drinking party in the Xinchang quarter, when
Zheng, who had some private business, left Wei south
of the Xuanping quarter, saying he would join him later
at the feast. Then Wei headed east on his white horse,
while Zheng rode south on his donkey through the north
gate of the Shengping quarter.

On the road Zheng came upon three girls, one of
whom, dressed in a white gown, was exceedingly lovely.
Pleasantly surprised, he whipped up his donkey to circle
round them, but lacked the courage to accost them.
Since the girl in white kept glancing at him in what
seemed an encouraging way, he asked jokingly:

Shen Jiji (c. 750-800) was a native of Suzhou and a good classical
scholar and historian. He is the author of *The Story of the Pillow*.

"Why should such beautiful girls as you travel on foot?"

The girl in white countered with a smile: "If men with mounts aren't polite enough to offer us a lift, what else can we do?"

"My poor donkey is not good enough for such lovely ladies as you," protested Zheng. "But it is at your disposal, and I shall be glad to follow you on foot."

He and the girl looked at each other and laughed, and with her two maids teasing them they were soon on familiar terms. He went east with these young women to Leyuan Park, and dusk had fallen by the time they reached a magnificent mansion with massive walls and an imposing gate. The girl in white went in, calling back over her shoulder, "Wait a little!" One of her maids stayed at the gate and asked Zheng his name. Having told her, he inquired the name of the girl and learned that her surname was Ren and that she was the twentieth child in the family.

Presently Zheng was invited in. He had just tethered his donkey at the gate and placed his hat on the saddle, when the girl's sister — a woman of thirty or thereabouts — came out to greet him. Candles were set out, the table spread, and they had drunk several cups of wine when the girl, who had changed her dress, joined them. Then they drank a great deal and made merry, and late at night they went to bed together. Her coquetry and charm, the way she sang and laughed and moved — it was all exquisite and something out of this world. Just before dawn Ren said, "You had better go now. My brother is a member of the royal conservatory of music and serves in the royal guards. He'll be home at daybreak and he mustn't see you." Having arranged to come again, Zheng left.

When he reached the end of the street, the gate of that quarter was still bolted. But there was a foreign bread shop there where a light was burning and the stove had been lit. Sitting under the awning, waiting for the morning drum, Zheng began chatting with the shopkeeper. Pointing to where he had spent the night, he asked, "When you turn east from here you come to a big gate — whose house is that?"

"It's all in ruins," said the shopkeeper. "There's no house left."

"But I was there," insisted Zheng. "How can you say there is no house?"

The shopkeeper understood in a flash what had happened. "Ah, now I see it!" he exclaimed. "There's a fox fairy there, who often tempts men to spend the night with her. She has been seen three times. So you met her too, did you?"

Ashamed to admit the truth, Zheng denied this. When it was light he looked at the place again, and found the walls and the gate still there, but only waste land and a deserted garden behind.

After reaching home he was blamed by Wei for not joining him the previous day; but instead of telling the truth, Zheng made up an excuse. He was still bewitched by the fairy's beauty, however, and longed to see her again, unable to drive her image from his heart. About a fortnight later, in a clothes shop in the West Market, he once more came upon her accompanied by her maids. When he called out to her, she tried to slip into the crowd to avoid him; but he called her name repeatedly and pushed forward. Then, with her back to him and her fan behind her, she said: "You know who I am. Why do you follow me?"

"What if I do?" asked Zheng.

"I feel ashamed to face you," she replied.

"I love you so much, how could you leave me?" he protested.

"I don't want to leave you; I'm only afraid you must hate me."

When Zheng swore that he still loved her and became more insistent in his request, the girl turned round and let fall the fan, appearing as dazzlingly beautiful as ever.

"There are many fox fairies about," she told the young man. "It's just that you don't know them for what they are. You needn't think it strange."

Zheng begged her to come back to him and she said, "Fox fairies have a bad name because they often harm men; but that is not my way. If I have not lost your favour, I would like to serve you all my life." Asked where they could live, she suggested, "East of here you'll come to a house with a big tree towering above its roof. It's in a quiet part of town — why not rent it? The other day when I first met you south of the Xuan-ping quarter, another gentleman rode off on a white horse towards the east. Wasn't he your brother-in-law? There's a lot of furniture in his house you can borrow."

It so happened, indeed, that Wei's uncles, absent on official duty, had stored away their furniture with him. Acting on Ren's advice, Zheng went to Wei and asked to borrow it. Asked the reason, he said, "I have just got a beautiful mistress and rented a house for her. I want to borrow the furniture for her use."

"A beauty, indeed!" retorted Wei with a laugh.

"Judging by your own looks, you must have found some monstrosity!"

None the less his friend lent him curtains, bed and bedding, dispatching an intelligent servant with him to have a look at the girl. Presently the servant ran back, out of breath and sweating. "Well?" asked Wei, stepping forward. "Have you seen her? What's she like?"

"Marvellous! I've never seen anyone so lovely!"

Wei, who had many relations and had seen many beauties in the course of his numerous adventures, asked whether Zheng's mistress was a match for one of these.

"No comparison!" exclaimed the servant. Wei mentioned four or fives other names, but still received a negative reply. His sister-in-law, sixth daughter of the Prince of Wu, was a peerless beauty, as lovely as a fairy. "How does she compare with the sixth daughter of the Prince of Wu?" he asked.

But again his man declared that there was no comparison.

"Is that possible?" Wei exclaimed, clasping his hands in amazement. Then he hastily asked for water to wash his neck, put on a new cap, rouged his lips and went to call on Zheng.

It happened that Zheng was out and Wei, entering, found a young servant sweeping and a maid at the door, but no one else. He questioned the boy, who told him with a laugh that there was no one at home. But making a search of the rooms, Wei saw a red skirt behind a door and going closer discovered Ren hiding there. Dragged out from the dark corner, she was even more beautiful than he had been told. Mad with passion, he took her in his arms to assault her, only to meet with resistance. He pressed her hard, until she said, "You shall have your way, but first let me recover my breath." However, when Wei came on again she resisted as before. This happened three or four times. Finally Wei held her down with all his strength and the girl, exhausted and drenched with perspiration, knew she could hardly escape. Limp and inert, she gave him a heart-rending look.

"Why are you so sad?" he asked.

With a long sigh, she answered, "I pity Zheng with all my heart."

"What do you mean?" he demanded.

"He's over six feet tall but has failed to protect a woman — how can he call himself a man? You are young and rich, and have many beautiful mistresses. You have seen many like me. But Zheng is a poor man, and I am the only woman he loves. How can you rob him of his only love while you have so many? Because he is poor, he has to be dependent on others. He wears your clothes, eats your food, and so he is in your power. If he could support himself, we shouldn't have come to this."

At this, Wei, a gallant man with a sense of justice, desisted, composed himself and apologized. Then Zheng came back and they exchanged cordial greetings. And thenceforward Wei looked after all their needs.

Ren often met Wei and went out with him on foot or by carriage. He spent almost every day with her until they became the best of friends, taking great delight in each other's company. And because she was everything to him except his mistress, he loved and respected her and grudged her nothing. Even eating and drinking he could not forget her. Knowing Wei's love for her, Ren said to him one day: "I'm ashamed to accept such favours from you. I don't deserve such kindness. And I can't betray Zheng to do as you desire. I was born in Shaanxi and brought up in the capital. My family are theatre people, and since all the women in it are the mistresses and concubines of rich men, they know every single courtesan in the capital. If you see some beautiful girl and cannot have her, I would like to get her for you to repay your kindness." Wei accepted her offer.

A dress-maker named Zhang in the market place took Wei's fancy with her clear complexion and fine figure. He asked Ren if she knew her, and she answered, "She is my cousin. I can get her easily." After about ten days, she brought this woman to him. A few months later, when Wei was tired of Zhang, Ren said, "Market girls are easy game. Try to think of someone most charming but hardly attainable, and I shall do my best for you."

"The other day at the Han Shi Festival,"* said Wei, "I went to Qianfu Temple with some friends when General Diao had brought his musicians to play in the hall. One of them was a reed-organ player, a girl of about sixteen with two locks of hair over her ears. She was charming — quite lovely! Do you know her?"

"She's the general's favourite," answered Ren. "Her mother is my sister. I'll see what I can do."

Wei bowed to her, and Ren promised him her help. She became a frequent visitor at the general's house. After a whole month had passed, Wei urged her to make haste and inquired what her plan was. She asked him for two bolts of silk to use as a bribe, and these

---

* On this day in early spring no stoves were lit and people ate cold food (han shi).

he gave to her. Two days later, he was having a meal with Ren when the general sent his steward with a black horse to beg her to go to his house. Hearing this summons, Ren smiled at Wei and said, "It is done!" It seemed that she had made the favourite fall ill with a disease which medicine was powerless to cure. At their wits' end, the girl's mother and the general had consulted a witch doctor; but Ren had shown this witch doctor her house and bribed her to say that the sick girl must be removed there.

Accordingly the witch doctor told the general, "The girl must not stay at home but should go and live in that house in the southeast, to imbibe the life-giving influences there." When they made inquiries and found it was Ren's house, the general asked her to let the girl lodge there. At first Ren declined, saying her house was too small, and only after repeated requests did she give her consent. Then the general sent the girl in a carriage with clothing and trinkets, accompanied by her mother, to Ren's house. As soon as she arrived, she was cured. Within a few days, Ren secretly introduced Wei to her, and a month later she was with child. But then her mother took fright, and carried her back hastily to the general; so this was the end of that affair.

One day Ren asked Zheng, "Can you lay your hands on five or six thousand coins? If so, I promise to make a profit for you."

When he had raised a loan of six thousand coins, she told him, "Go to the horse-dealers in the market. You will find a horse with a spot on its rump — buy it and take it home."

Zheng went to the market where he saw a man trying to sell a horse which, sure enough, had a black mark on its rump. Accordingly he bought it and led it home. His brothers-in-law scoffed, "Nobody wants a hack like that. What did you buy such a crock for?"

Soon after that, Ren told him: "The time has come to sell the horse. You should get thirty thousand for it." Then Zheng took the horse to the market, and was offered twenty thousand but refused to sell.

All the folk in the market marvelled: "Why does one offer such a price? Why does the other refuse to sell?"

When Zheng started to ride away, the would-be purchaser followed him to the gate and raised his offer to twenty-five thousand, but still Zheng would not sell. "Nothing doing under thirty thousand," he declared. Then, however, his brothers-in-law gathered round and pestered him into selling at just under thirty thousand.

Later he found out the reason for the buyer's insistence: This man was the groom of Zhaoying County, and one of his horses which had a black mark on its rump had died three years before. This fellow was to be discharged soon, and was due to be paid sixty thousand for keeping the horses. If he could buy a horse for half that sum and hand it over to the government, he would still be the gainer. He would be paid for three years' fodder which had never been consumed. That was why he had insisted on buying.

Once Ren asked Wei for some new dresses, as her old gowns were worn out. He wanted to buy silk for her, but she declined, saying she preferred ready-made clothes. Wei commissioned a shopkeeper named Zhang to get them, sending him to Ren to find out just what she wanted. When the shopkeeper saw her, he was so astonished that later he said to Wei, "That is no common woman, she must be from some noble house. It isn't right for you to keep her. I hope you will return her to her family soon, to avoid trouble." This shows how striking her appearance was.

However, they could not understand why she insisted on buying ready-made dresses instead of having them made to measure.

A year later Zheng was appointed a captain of Huaili Prefecture, with his headquarters at Jincheng. Now since Zheng had a wife, though he spent the day with his mistress he had to go home to sleep at night, and he missed Ren. So when he was going to his post he asked her to accompany him; but she refused.

"We should only be together for a month or two," she said. "It seems hardly worth it. It would be better to work out how much I shall need to spend while you're away, and let me wait at home till you come back." Although Zheng pleaded with her, she was adamant. Then Zheng asked Wei for a loan, and Wei came to persuade her too and to ask the reason. After some little hesitation she answered, "A witch told me it would be unlucky for me to go west this year. That's why I want to stay here."

But Zheng was so eager for her to go, he could think of nothing else. Both men laughed at her and demanded, "How can an intelligent girl like you be so superstitious?" They reasoned with her.

"If what the witch said was true," said Ren, "and I die because I go with you, won't you be sorry?"

"Nonsense!" declared the two men, and insisted again. Finally they persuaded her against her will.

Wei lent her his horse and saw them off at Lingao. The next day they reached Mawei. Ren was riding ahead on the horse with Zheng behind on his donkey,

followed by her maid and other attendants. The game-
keepers outside the West Gate had been training their
hounds at Luochuan for some ten days, and just as Ren
was passing the hounds leaped out from the bushes.
Then Zheng saw his mistress drop to the ground, turn
into a fox and fly southwards with the pack in hot pur-
suit. He ran forward and yelled at the hounds, but could
not restrain them; and after running a few hundred
yards she was caught. Shedding tears, Zheng took money
from his pocket to buy back the carcass, which was then
buried with a pointed stick stuck into the ground to mark
the place. When he looked back, her horse was cropping
grass by the roadside, her clothes were lying on the
saddle, while her shoes and stockings were hanging on
the stirrups like the skin shed by a cicada. Her trinkets
had dropped to the ground, but everything else belong-
ing to her had vanished, including her maid.

About ten days later Zheng returned to the capital.
Wei was delighted to see him, and coming forward to
greet him asked, "Is Ren well?"

With tears Zheng replied, "She is dead!"

Wei was stricken with grief at this news. They embraced each other and mourned bitterly, then Wei asked
what sudden illness had carried her off.

"She was killed by hounds," answered Zheng.

"Even fierce hounds cannot kill men," protested
Wei.

"But she was no human being."

When Wei cried out in amazement, his friend told
him the whole story. He could only marvel and heave
sigh after sigh. The next day they went together by
carriage to Mawei, and after opening the grave to look
at the carcass returned prostrated with grief. When they

thought back over her behaviour, the only unusual habit they could recall was that she would never have her clothes made to measure.

Later Zheng became the inspector of the royal stable and a very wealthy man, keeping a stable of some dozen horses. He·died at the age of sixty-five.

During the Da Li period (766-779), I was staying at Zhongling and spent much time with Wei, who told me ·this story over and over again until I knew it inside out. Later Wei became a chancellor of the imperial court and concurrently Prefect of Longzhou, finally dying at his post in the northwest.

It is sad to think that a beast assuming human form should resist violation and remain chaste and faithful to her lord till death, while few women nowadays are equal to this! And what a pity that Zheng was not more intelligent. He simply appreciated her appearance without studying her nature. A really wise man would have probed the laws of change, investigated the nature of supernatural beings, and with his skilful pen recorded the gist of the mystery, instead of simply contenting himself with the enjoyment of her grace and charm. This is most unfortunate!

In the second year of the Jian Zhong period (AD 781), when I was Left Adviser, I left for Suzhou at the same time that General Bei Qi, Junior City Magistrate Sun Cheng, Minister Cui Xu of the Civil Affairs Ministry, and Right Adviser Lu Chun were setting out to the Yangtse Valley. We travelled together from the province of Shaanxi to Suzhou by land and along the waterways. With us too was ex-Adviser Zhu Fang, who was on a tour. As we floated down the Ying and Huai

Rivers in our boat, feasting by day and conversing at night, each of us told of some strange happenings. When these gentlemen heard the story of Ren, they were deeply moved and greatly astonished; and because they asked me to record this strange tale, I have written this narrative.

The Dragon King's Daughter

Li Chaowei

DURING the Yi Feng period (676-678), a scholar named Liu Yi failed in the official examination and, as he
was returning to the Xiang River Valley, decided to go
and take his leave of a fellow provincial who was staying at Jingyang. He had ridden about two miles, when
a bird flying up from the ground startled his horse and
made it bolt and it had galloped two miles before he
could stop it. Then he caught sight of a girl herding
sheep by the roadside. She was amazingly beautiful
but her finely arched eyebrows were knit, her clothes
were soiled, and she was standing there listening intently as if awaiting someone's arrival.

"What has brought you to such a wretched state?"
Liu asked.

The girl first expressed her gratitude with a smile;
then, unable to restrain her tears, replied, "Unhappy
creature that I am! Since you ask me the reason, how
can I hide the deep resentment I feel? Listen then! I
am the youngest daughter of the dragon king of Dongting Lake. My parents married me to the second son of
the dragon king of the Jing River; but my husband,

Li Chaowei (c. 800) was a native of Longxi (present-day Gansu
province).

devoted to pleasure and led astray by his attendants, treated me more unkindly every day. I complained to his parents, but they were too fond of their son to take my part. When I persisted in complaining, they grew angry and banished me here." Having said this, she broke down and sobbed.

"Dongting Lake is so far away," she went on. "It lies beyond the distant horizon, and I can get no word to my family. My heart is breaking and my eyes are worn out with watching, but there is no one to know my grief or pity me. Since you are going south and will pass near the lake, may I trouble you to take a letter?"

"I have a sense of justice," answered Liu, "and your story makes my blood boil. I only wish I had wings to fly there — why talk of trouble? But the lake is very deep, and I can only walk on land. How am I to convey your message? I fear I may be unable to get through, proving unworthy of your trust and failing in my own sincere wish to help you. Can you tell me how to make the journey?"

"I cannot say how I appreciate your kindness," said the girl, shedding tears. "If ever I receive a reply, I shall repay you even if it costs my life. Before you promised to help me, I dared not tell you how to reach my parents; but actually, to go to the lake is no harder than going to the capital."

Asked for directions, she told him, "South of the lake stands a big orange tree which is the sacred tree of the village. Take off this belt, put on another, and knock on the trunk three times. Someone will come to your call, and if you follow him you will have no difficulty. I have opened my heart to you besides trusting you with my letter. Please tell my parents what you have heard. On no account fail me!"

Liu promised to do as she said. Then the girl took a letter from her pocket and handed it to him with a bow, all the while looking eastwards and weeping in a way that touched his heart.

When he had put the letter in his wallet, he inquired, "May I ask why you herd sheep? Do deities also eat cattle?"

"No," she answered. "These are not sheep, but rain-bringers."

"What are they?"

"Thunder, lightning, and the like."

Liu looked at the sheep closely, and saw that they moved proudly with heads held high. They cropped the grass differently too, although they were the same size as ordinary sheep and had the same wool and horns.

"Now that I am going to act as your messenger," he said, "I hope in future, when you get back to the lake, you won't refuse to see me."

"Certainly not!" she exclaimed. "I shall treat you as a dear relative."

Then they bid each other goodbye, and he started east. After a few dozen yards he looked back, but both girl and sheep had disappeared.

That evening he reached the county town and said goodbye to his friend. It took him over a month to get home, and he went without delay to Dongting Lake. He found the orange tree south of the lake, changed his belt, faced the tree and knocked three times. A warrior came out of the water, and bowed to him. "Why have you come here, honourable sir?" he asked.

Without telling him the story, Liu simply answered, "To see your king."

The warrior parted the waves and pointed the way, saying to Liu as he led him down, "Close your eyes. We will be there in no time."

Liu did as he was told, and soon they reached a great palace where he saw clustered towers and pavilions, millions of gates and arches, and all the rare plants and trees of the world. The warrior asked him to wait at the corner of a great hall.

"What place is this?" asked Liu.

"The Palace of the Divine Void."

Looking round, Liu saw that this palace was filled with every precious object known to man. The pillars were of white jade, the steps of jasper; the couches were of coral, the screens of crystal. The emerald lintels were set with cut glass, while the rainbow-coloured beams were inlaid with amber. And the whole created an impression of strange beauty and unfathomable depth which defied description.

The dragon king was a long time in coming, and Liu asked the warrior, "Where is the Lord of Dongting?"

"His Majesty is in the Dark Pearl Pavilion," was the reply. "He is discussing the Fire Canon with the Sun Priest, but will have finished soon."

"What is the Fire Canon?" Liu wanted to know.

"Our king is a dragon," was the reply, "so water is his element, and with one drop of water he can flood mountains and valleys. The priest is a man, so fire is his element, and with one torch he can burn down a whole palace. Since the properties of the elements differ, they have different effects. As the Sun Priest is expert in the laws of men, our king has asked him over for a talk."

He had barely finished speaking when the palace gate opened, a mist seemed to gather and there appeared a man in purple holding a jasper sceptre. The warrior leaped to attention, crying, "This is our king!" Then he went forward to report Liu's arrival.

The dragon king looked at Liu and asked, "Are you not of the world of men?"

Liu replied that he was, and bowed. The king greeted him in return and asked him to be seated.

"Our watery kingdom is dark and deep, and I am ignorant," said the dragon king. "What has brought you, sir, from such a distance?"

"I am of the same district as Your Majesty," replied Liu. "I was born in the south, but have studied in the northwest. Not long ago, after failing in the examination, I was riding by the Jing River when I came upon your daughter herding sheep in the open country. Exposed to wind and rain, she was a pitiful sight. When questioned, she told me she had come to such a pass because of her husband's unkindness and his parents' neglect. I assure you, her tears as she spoke went to my heart. Then she entrusted this letter to me and I promised to deliver it. That is why I am here." He took out the letter and passed it to the king.

After reading the missive, the king covered up his face and wept. "Though I am her old father," he lamented, "I have been like a man blind and deaf, unaware that my child was suffering far away, while you, a stranger, came to her rescue. As long as I live, I shall never forget your kindness." He gave way to weeping, and all the attendants shed tears.

Presently a palace eunuch approached the king, who handed him the letter with orders to tell the women in the inner palace. Soon wailing was heard from within and in alarm the king bade his attendants, "Quickly tell the women not to make so much noise, or the Prince of Qiantang may hear them!"

"Who is this prince?" asked Liu.

"My younger brother," said the dragon king. "He used to be the Prince of the Qiantang River, but has now retired."

"Why must you keep it from him?"

"Because he is overbold," was the reply. "The nine years of flood in the time of the ancient sage King Yao was due to one of his rages. Not long ago he quarrelled with the angels in heaven and flooded the five mountains. Thanks to a few good deeds I had to my credit, the heavenly emperor pardoned him; but he has to be kept here. The people of Qiantang are waiting still for his return."

He had scarcely finished when there came a great crash, as if both heaven and earth had been torn asunder. The palace shook and mist seethed as in burst a crimson dragon more than a thousand feet long, dragging after it a jade pillar to which its neck had been fastened by a gold chain. Its eyes were bright as lightning, its tongue red as blood, and it had scarlet scales and a fiery mane. Thunder crashed and lightning flashed around it, then snow and hail fell thick and fast, after which it soared up into the azure sky.

Panic-stricken, Liu had fallen to the ground. But now the king himself helped him up, urging, "Have no fear! All is well."

After a long time, Liu recovered a little. And when

calm enough he asked leave to withdraw. "I had better go while I can," he explained. "I couldn't survive another experience like that."

"There's no need to leave," said the king. "That's the way my brother goes, but he won't come back that way. Do stay a little longer." He called for wine, and they drank to pledge their friendship.

Then a soft breeze sprang up, wafting over auspicious clouds. Amid flying pennons and flags and the sound of flutes and pipes, in came thousands of brightly dressed, laughing and chattering girls. Among them was one with beautiful, arched eyebrows who was wearing bright jewels and a gown of the finest gauze. When she drew near, Liu saw that she was the girl who had given him the message. Now she was shedding tears of joy, as she moved through a fragrant red and purple mist to the inner palace.

The king said with a laugh to Liu, "Here comes the prisoner from the Jing River!" He excused himself and went inside, and from the inner palace happy weeping was heard. Then the king came out again to feast with Liu.

Presently a man in purple strode up to stand by the king. He was holding a jasper sceptre and looked vigorous and full of spirit. The king introduced him as the Prince of Qiantang.

Liu stood up to bow, and the prince bowed in return. "My unhappy niece was insulted by that young blackguard," he said. "It was good of you, sir, with your strong sense of justice, to carry the news of her wrongs so far. If not for you, she would have pined away by the Jing River. No words can express our gratitude."

Liu bowed and thanked him. Then the prince told his brother, "I reached the river in one hour, fought there for another hour, and took another hour to come back. On my return journey I flew to high heaven to report to the Heavenly Emperor; and when he knew the injustice done he pardoned me. In fact, he pardoned my past faults as well. But I am thoroughly ashamed that in my indignation I did not stop to say goodbye, upsetting the whole palace and alarming our honourable guest." He bowed again.

"How many did you kill?" asked the king.

"Six hundred thousand."

"Did you destroy any fields?"

"About three hundred miles."

"Where is that scoundrel, her husband?"

"I ate him."

The king looked pained.

"Of course that young blackguard was insufferable," he said. "Still, that was going rather far. It is lucky that the Heavenly Emperor is omniscient and pardoned you because such a great injustice had been done. Otherwise what could I have said in your defence? Don't ever do that again!" The prince bowed once more.

That evening Liu was lodged in the Hall of Frozen Light, and the next day another feast was given at the Emerald Palace. All the royal family gathered there, music was played, and wine and delicacies were served. Then bugles, horns and drums sounded as ten thousand warriors danced with flags, swords and halberds on the right-hand side, while one came forward to announce that this was the triumphal march of the Prince of Qiantang. This spectacular and awe-inspiring display impressed all who saw it.

Then to an accompaniment of gongs and cymbals, stringed and bamboo instruments, a thousand girls dressed in bright silks and decked with jewels danced on the left-hand side, while one came forward to announce that this music was to celebrate the return of the princess. The melodies were poignant and sweet, breathing such grief and longing that all who heard were moved to tears. When the two dances were over, the dragon king in high good humour made the dancers presents of silk. Then the guests sat down together to feast, and drank to their hearts' content.

When they had drunk their fill, the king rapped on the table and sang:

> *Wide the earth and grey the sky,*
> *Who can hear a distant cry?*
> *The fox lies snugly in his lair,*
> *But thunderbolts can reach him there.*
> *A true man, who upholds the right,*
> *Restored my daughter to my sight.*
> *Such service how can we requite?*

After the king's song ended, the prince made a bow and sang:

> *Life and death are fixed by fate,*
> *Our princess found a worthless mate.*
> *By River Jing she had to go,*
> *In wind and frost, in rain and snow.*
> *This gentleman her letter bore,*
> *Then we restored her to this shore.*
> *This we'll remember evermore!*

After this song, the king and prince stood up and

each presented a cup to Liu, who hesitated bashfully before accepting, then quaffed off the wine, returned the cups and sang:

> *Like a blossom in the rain,*
> *The princess longed for home in vain,*
> *I brought back tidings of her plight,*
> *And all her wrongs were soon set right,*
> *Now we feast, but soon must part,*
> *For home again I needs must start.*
> *Bitter longing fills my heart!*

This song of his was greeted by loud applause.

The king brought out a jasper casket of rhinoceros horn which could part the waves, and the prince an amber dish bearing jade that shone at night. They presented these to Liu, who accepted the gifts with thanks. Then the inmates of the palace started piling silk and jewels beside him, until gorgeous materials were heaped up all around. Laughing and chatting with the company, he had not a moment's quiet. Sated at last with wine and pleasure, he excused himself and went back to sleep in the Hall of Frozen Light.

The next day he was feasting again in the Pavilion of Limpid Light when the Prince of Qiantang, heated with wine and lounging on the couch, said insolently, "A hard rock can be smashed but not made to yield, and a gallant man can be killed but not put to shame. I have a proposal to make. If you agree, all will be well between us. If not, we can perish together. How about it?"

"Let me hear your proposal," said Liu.

"As you know, the wife of the Lord of the Jing River

is our sovereign's daughter," said the prince. "She is an excellent girl with a fine character, well thought of by all her kinsmen but unlucky enough to have suffered indignities at the hands of that scoundrel. However, that's a thing of the past. We would like to entrust her to you, and become your relatives for ever. Then she who owes you gratitude will belong to you, and we who love her will know she is in good hands. A generous man shouldn't do things by halves. Don't you agree?"

For a moment Liu looked grave. Then he rejoined with a laugh, "I never thought the Prince of Qiantang would have such unworthy ideas. I have heard that once when you crossed the nine continents, you shook the five mountains to give vent to your anger; and I have seen you break the golden chain and drag the jade pillar after you to rescue your niece. I thought there was no one as brave and just as you, who dared risk death to right a wrong, and would sacrifice your life for those you love. These are the true marks of greatness. Yet now, while music is being played and host and guest are in harmony, you try to force me to do your will in defiance of honour. I would never have expected this of you! If I met you on the angry sea or among dark mountains, with your fins and beard flying and mist and rain all around, though you threatened me with death I should consider you a mere beast and not count it against you. But now you are in human garb. You talk of manners and show a profound understanding of human relationships and the ways of men. You have a nicer sense of propriety than many gallants in the world of men, not to say monsters of the deep. Yet you try to use your strength and temper — while pretending to be drunk — to force me to agree to your proposal.

This is hardly right. Although small enough to hide under one of your scales, I am not afraid of your anger. I hope you will reconsider your proposal."

Then the prince apologized. "Brought up in the palace, I was never taught etiquette," he said. "Just now I spoke wildly and offended you — your rebuke was well deserved. Don't let this spoil our friendship." That night they feasted together again as merrily as ever, and Liu and the prince became great friends.

The day after, Liu asked permission to leave. The queen gave another feast for him in the Hall of Hidden Light, which was attended by a great throng of men and women, maids and servants. Shedding tears, the queen said to him, "My daughter owes you so much, we can never repay you. And we are sorry to have to say goodbye." She told the princess to thank him.

"Shall we ever meet again?" asked the queen.

Liu regretted now that he had not agreed to the prince's request. His heart was very heavy. After the feast, when he bid them farewell, the whole palace was filled with sighing, and countless rare jewels were given him as parting gifts.

He left the lake by the way he had come, escorted by a dozen or more attendants who carried his bags to his home before leaving him. He went to a jeweller's at Yangzhou to sell some of the jewels, and though he parted with about one hundredth only he became a multi-millionaire, wealthier by far than all the rich men west of the Huai River.

He married a girl called Zhang, but soon she died. Then he married a girl called Han; but after several months she died as well, and Liu moved to Nanjing.

Loneliness tempted him to marry again, and a go-

between told him, "There is a girl called Lu from Fan-
yang County, whose father, Lu Hao, used to be
magistrate of Qingliu. In his later years he studied
Taoist philosophy and lived by himself in the wilder-
ness, so that now no one knows where he is. Her mother
was named Zheng. The year before last the girl married into the Zhang family at Qinghe, but unfortunately
her husband died. Because she is young, intelligent and
beautiful, her mother wants to find a good husband for
her. Are you interested?"

So Liu married this girl on an auspicious day, and
since both families were wealthy, the magnificence of
their gifts and equipage impressed the whole city of
Nanjing.

Coming home one evening about a month after their
marriage, Liu was struck by his wife's resemblance to
the dragon king's daughter, except that she was in better health and more lovely. Accordingly, he told her
what had happened.

"I can't believe it," she replied. Then she told him
that she was with child, and Liu became more devoted
to her than ever.

A month after the child was born, Liu's wife dressed
herself in fine clothes, put on her jewels, and invited
all their relatives to the house. Before the assembled
company she asked him with a smile, "Don't you remember meeting me before?"

"Once I carried a message for the dragon king's
daughter," he replied. "That is something I have never
forgotten."

"I am the dragon king's daughter," she said. "Wronged by my former husband, I was rescued by you, and I
swore to repay your kindness. But when my uncle the

prince suggested that we marry, you refused. After our separation we lived in two different spheres, and I had no way of sending word to you. Later my parents wanted to marry me to another river god — that stripling of the Zhuoqin River — but I remained true to you. Although you had forsaken me and there was no hope of seeing you again, I would rather have died than stop loving you. Soon after that, my parents took pity on me and decided to approach you again; but you married girls from the Zhang and Han families, and there was nothing we could do. After those girls had died and you came to live here, my family felt the match was possible. But I never dared hope that one day I might be your wife. I shall be grateful and happy all my life, and die without regret." So saying, she wept.

Presently she went on: "I did not disclose myself to you before, because I knew you did not care for my looks. But I can tell you now that I know you are attached to me. I am not good enough to keep your love, so I'm counting on your fondness for the child to hold you. Before I knew you loved me, I was so anxious and worried! When you took my letter, you smiled at me and said, 'When you go back to the lake, don't refuse to see me!' Did you want us to become husband and wife in future? Later when my uncle proposed the marriage and you refused him, did you really mean it or were you just offended? Do tell me!"

"It must have been fated," said Liu. "When first I met you by the river, you looked so wronged and pale, my heart bled for you. But I think all I wanted at the time was to pass on your message and right your wrong. When I said I hoped you wouldn't refuse to see me in future, that was just a casual remark with nothing be-

hind it. The prince's attempt to force me into marriage annoyed me because I object to being bullied.
Since a sense of justice had motivated my action, I
could hardly marry the woman whose husband's death
I had caused. As a man of honour I had to do what
I thought right. So during our drinking I spoke from
my heart, saying only what was just, with no fear of
him. Once the time came to leave, however, and I
saw the regret in your eyes, I was rather sorry. But
after I left the lake, the affairs of this world kept me
too occupied to convey my love and gratitude to you.
Well, now that you belong to the Lu family and are a
woman, I find my former feelings towards you were
more than a fleeting passion after all! From now on,
I shall love you always."

His wife was deeply moved and replied with tears,
"Don't think human beings alone know gratitude. I
shall repay your kindness. A dragon lives for ten
thousand years, and I shall share my span of life with
you. We shall travel freely by land and sea. You
can trust me."

"I never thought you could tempt me with immortality!" laughed Liu.

They went to the lake again, where the royal enter-
tainment once more given them beggars description.

Later they lived at Nanhai for forty years. Their mansions, equipage, feasts and clothes were as splendid as
those of a prince, and Liu was able to help all his relatives. His perennial youth amazed everybody. During
the Kai Yuan period (AD 713-741), when the emperor
set his heart on discovering the secret of long life and
searched far and wide for alchemists, Liu was given no
peace and went back with his wife to the lake. Thus

he disappeared from the world for more than ten years. At the end of that period, his younger cousin, Xue Gu, lost his post as magistrate of the capital and was sent to the southeast. On his journey Xue crossed Dongting Lake. It was a clear day and he was looking into the distance when he saw a green mountain emerging from the distant waves. The boatmen shrank back in fear, crying, "There was never any mountain here — it must be a sea monster!"

As they were watching the mountain approach, a painted barge came swiftly towards them and the men on it called Xue's name. One of them told him, "Master Liu sends his greetings." Then Xue understood. Invited to the foot of the mountain, he picked up the skirt of his gown and went quickly ashore. On the mountain were palaces like those on earth, and Liu was standing there with musicians before and bejewelled girls behind him, more splendid than in the world of men. Talking more brilliantly and looking even younger than formerly, he greeted Xue at the steps and took his hand.

"We have not been separated long," he said, "yet your hair is turning grey."

"You are fated to become an immortal and I to become dry bones," retorted Xue with a laugh.

Liu gave him fifty capsules, and said, "Each of these will give you an extra year of life. When you have finished them, come again. Don't stay too long in the world of men, where you must undergo so many hardships." They feasted happily, and then Xue left. Liu was never seen again, but Xue often related this story. And fifty years later, he too vanished from the world.

This tale shows that the principal species of each category* of living creatures possesses supernatural powers — for how otherwise could reptiles assume the virtues of men? The dragon king of Dongting showed himself truly magnanimous, while the Prince of Qiantang was impetuous and straightforward. Surely their virtues did not appear from nowhere. Liu's cousin, Xue Gu, was the only other human being to penetrate to that watery kingdom, and it is a pity that none of his writings have been preserved. But since this account holds such interest, I have recorded it here.

---

* The ancient Chinese divided the animal kingdom into five categories: feathered, furred, hard-shelled, scaly and hairless. The chief species of these categories were phoenix, unicorn, tortoise, dragon and man. From man, the most intelligent of all, these others derived some of their virtues.

Prince Huo's Daughter

Jiang Fang

DURING the Da Li period (766-779), there was a young man of Longxi whose name was Li Yi. At the age of twenty he passed one of the civil service examinations and the following year the best scholars of his rank were to be chosen for official posts through a further examination at the Ministry of Civil Affairs. In the sixth month he arrived at the capital and took lodgings in the Xinchang quarter. He came from a good family, showed brilliant promise, and was acknowledged by his contemporaries as unsurpassed in literary craftsmanship. Thus even senior scholars looked up to him. Having no mean opinion of his own gifts, he hoped for a beautiful and accomplished wife. But long and vainly did he search among the famous courtesans of the capital.

In Chang'an there was a match-maker named Bao, who was the eleventh child in her family. She had been a maidservant in the prince consort's family, but a dozen years before this had redeemed herself and married. Clever and with a ready tongue, she knew all the great families and was a past master at arranging matches.

Jiang Fang lived at the beginning of the ninth century. He has left a volume of poetry as well as this story which won him fame.

Li gave her rich gifts and asked her to find him a wife, and she was very well disposed towards him.

One afternoon, some months later, Li was sitting in the south pavilion of his lodgings when he heard insistent knocking and Bao was announced. Gathering up the skirt of his gown, he hurried to meet her. "What brings you here so unexpectedly, madam?" he asked.

Bao laughed and responded, "Have you been having sweet dreams? A fairy has come down to earth who cares nothing for wealth but who admires wit and gallantry. She is made for you!"

When Li heard this he leaped for joy and felt as if he were walking on air. Taking Bao's hand he bowed and thanked her, saying: "I shall be your slave as long as I live!"

Asked where the girl lived and what her name was, Bao replied: "She is the youngest daughter of Prince Huo. Her name is Jade, and the prince doted on her. Her mother, Qinchi, was his favourite slave. When the prince died, his sons refused to keep the child because her mother was of humble birth, so they gave her a portion and made her leave. She has changed her name to Zheng, and people do not know that the prince was her father. But she is the most beautiful creature you ever saw, with a sensibility and grace beyond compare. She is well versed too in music and the classics. Yesterday she asked me to find a good match for her, and when I mentioned your name she was delighted, for she knows you by reputation. They live in Old Temple Lane in the Shengye quarter, in the house at the entrance to the carriage drive. I have already made an appointment for you. Go tomorrow at noon to the end of the lane, and look for a maid called Guizi. She will show you the house."

As soon as the match-maker left, Li started to prepare for the great occasion, sending his servant Qiuhong to borrow a black charger with a gilt bit from his cousin Shang who was adjutant general of the capital. That evening he washed his clothes, had a bath, and shaved. He could not sleep all night for joy. At dawn he put on his cap and examined himself in the mirror, fearing all might not go well. Having frittered away the time till noon, he called for the horse and galloped to the Shengye quarter. When he reached the place appointed, he saw a maid standing there waiting for him, who asked, "Are you Master Li?" He dismounted, told the maid to stable the horse, and went quickly in, bolting the gate behind him.

The match-maker came out from the house, smiling at him from a distance as she cried, "Who is this gate-crasher?" While they were joking with each other, he found himself led through the inner gate into a court-yard where there were four cherry trees and a parrot cage hanging on the northwest side.

At the sight of Li, the parrot squawked, "Here's a guest! Lower the curtain!"

Naturally bashful, Li had felt some scruples about going in, and now the parrot startled him and brought him to a standstill until Bao led the girl's mother down the steps to welcome him, and he was asked to go inside and take a seat opposite her. The mother, little more than forty, was a slender, attractive woman with charming manners.

"We have heard of your brilliance as a scholar," she said to Li, "and now that I see what a handsome young man you are too, I am sure your fame is well deserved. I have a daughter who, though lacking in education, is not ill-favoured. She should be a suitable match for you. Madame Bao has already proposed this, and to-day I would like to offer my daughter to you in marriage."

"I am a clumsy fellow," he replied, "and do not deserve such a distinction. If you accept me, I shall count it a great honour as long as I live."

Then a feast was laid, Jade was called by her mother from the east chamber, and Li bowed to greet her. At her entrance, he felt as if the room had been transformed into a bower of roses, and when their eyes met he was dazzled by her glance. The girl sat down beside her mother, who said to her, "You like to repeat those lines:

> *When the wind in the bamboos rustles the*
>   *curtain,*
> *I fancy my old friend is near.'*

Here is the author of the poem. You have been reading his works so often — what do you think of him now you see him?"

Jade lowered her head and answered with a smile: "He doesn't live up to my expectations. Shouldn't a poet be more handsome?"

Then Li got up and made several bows. "You love talent and I admire beauty," he said. "Between us we have both!"

Jade and her mother looked at each other and smiled.

When they had drunk several cups of wine together, Li stood up and asked the girl to sing. At first she

declined, but her mother insisted, and in a clear voice
she sang an intricate melody. By the time they had
drunk their fill it was evening, and the match-maker
led the young man to the west wing to rest. The rooms
were secluded in a quiet courtyard, and the hangings
were magnificent. Bao told the maids Guizi and
Wansha to take off Li's boots and belt. Then Jade
herself appeared. With sweet archness and charming
coyness she put off her clothes. Then they lowered
the bed-curtains, lay down on the pillows and enjoyed
each other to their hearts' content. The young man felt
that he was in bed with a goddess.

During the night, however, the girl suddenly gazed at
him through tears and said, "As a courtesan, I know
I am no match for you. You love me now for my
looks, but I fear that when I lose them your feelings
will change, and then I shall be like a vine with nothing
to cling to, or a fan discarded in the autumn. So at the
height of my joy I cannot help grieving."

Li was touched, and putting his arm round her neck
said gently, "Today I have attained the dream of my
life. I swear I would sooner die than leave you. Why
do you talk like that? Let me have some white silk
to pledge you my faith in writing."

Drying her tears, Jade called her maid Yingtao to
raise the curtain and hold the candle, while she gave
Li a brush and ink. When not occupied with music,
Jade was fond of reading, and her writing-case, brushes
and ink all came from the palace. Now she brought out
an embroidered case and from it took three feet of
white silk lined with black for him to write on. The
young man had a gift for contemporary composition, and
taking up the brush wrote rapidly. He swore by the

mountains and rivers, by the sun and the moon, that he would be true. He wrote passionately and movingly, and when he had finished he gave Jade his pledge to keep in her jewel box.

After that they lived happily for two years like a pair of kingfishers soaring on high, together day and night. But in the spring of the third year, Li came first in his examination and was appointed secretary-general of Zheng County. In the fourth month, before leaving to take up his post and to visit his parents in Luoyang, he gave a farewell party to all his relatives at the capital. It was the season between spring and summer. When the feast was over and the guests had gone, the young man and the girl were filled with grief at their coming separation.

"With your talents and fame," said Jade, "you have many admirers who would like to be related to you by marriage. And your old parents at home have no daughter-in-law to look after them. So when you go to take up this post, you are bound to find a good wife. The pledge you made me is not binding. But I have a small request to make, which I hope you will consider. May I tell you what it is?"

Li was startled and protested, "In what way have I offended you, that you speak like this? Tell me what is in your mind, and I promise to do whatever you ask."

"I am eighteen," said the girl, "and you are only twenty-two. There are still eight years before you reach thirty, the age at which a man should marry. I would like to crowd into these eight years all the love and happiness of my life. After that you can choose some girl of good family for a wife — it will not be too late. Then I shall retire from the world, cutting my hair short

and becoming a nun.   This is the wish of my life and
I ask no more."

Cut to the heart, Li could not hold back his tears. "I
swear by the bright sun," he assured the girl, "as long
as I live I shall be true to you.   My only fear is that
I may fail to please you — how can I think of anything else?   I beg you not to doubt me, but rest assured.   I shall reach Huazhou in the eighth month and
send to fetch you.   We shall be together again before
very long." A few days later he said goodbye to her and
went east.

Ten days after Li's arrival at his post, he asked leave
to go to Luoyang to see his parents. Before he reached
home, his mother had arranged a match for him with
a cousin in the Lu family — a verbal agreement had already been reached.   His mother was so strict that Li,
though hesitating, dared not decline; accordingly he
went through with the ceremonies and arranged a date
for the wedding. Since the girl's family was a powerful
one, they demanded over a million cash betrothal money
and would call off the marriage if this were not forth-
coming.   Because Li's family was poor he had to borrow this sum; and he took advantage of his leave to
look up distant friends, travelling up and down the Huai
and Yangtse River valleys from the autumn till the
next summer. Knowing that he had broken his promise
to fetch Jade at the appointed time, he sent no message
to her, hoping that she would give him up. He also asked his friends not to disclose the truth.

When Li failed to return at the appointed time, Jade
tried to find out what had become of him, only to receive
contradictory reports.   She also consulted many fortune-
tellers and oracles. This went on for more than a year,

until at last she fell ill of sorrow; and, lying in her lonely room, went from bad to worse. Though no tidings had come from Li, her love for him did not falter, and she gave presents to friends and acquaintances to persuade them to find news of him. This she did so persistently that soon all her money had gone and she often had to send her maid out secretly to sell dresses and trinkets through an innkeeper in the West Market.

One day Jade sent Wansha to sell an amethyst hairpin, and on her way to the inn the maid met an old jade-smith who worked in the palace. When he saw what she was carrying, he recognized it. "This hair-pin is one I made," he said. "Many years ago, when Prince Huo's youngest daughter first put up her hair, he ordered me to make this pin and gave me ten thousand cash for the job. I have always remembered it. Who are you? And how did you come by this?"

"My mistress is the prince's daughter," replied the maid. "She has come down in the world, and the man she married went to Luoyang and deserted her. So she fell ill of grief, and has been in a decline for two years. Now she wants me to sell this, so that she can bribe someone to get news of her husband."

The jade-smith shed tears, exclaiming, "Can the children of nobles fall on such evil times? My days are nearly spent, but this ill-fated lady's story wrings my heart."

Then the old man led Wansha to the house of Princess Yanxian, and when the princess heard this story she too heaved sigh after sigh. Finally she gave the maid one hundred and twenty thousand cash for the hair-pin.

Now the girl to whom Li was engaged was in the capital. After raising the sum he needed for his marriage, he returned to his post in Zheng County; but at the end of the year he again asked for leave to go to Chang'an to get married. And he found quiet lodgings, so that his whereabouts would not be known. A young scholar, however, named Cui Yunming, who was Li's cousin and a kind-hearted man, had formerly drunk with Li in Jade's room and laughed and talked with her until they were on the best of terms. Whenever he received news of Li, he would tell Jade truthfully, and she had helped him so often with money and clothing that he felt deeply indebted to her.

When Li came to the capital, Cui told Jade, who sighed and exclaimed indignantly, "How can he be so faithless?" She begged all her friends to ask Li to come to her; but knowing that he had broken his promise and that the girl was dying, he felt too ashamed to see her. He took to going out early and coming back late in order to avoid callers. Though Jade wept day and night, unable to eat or sleep in her longing to see him, he never came. And indignation and grief made her illness worse. When the story became known in the capital, all the young scholars were moved by the girl's love while all the young gallants resented Li's heartlessness.

It was then spring, the season for pleasure trips, and Li went one day with five or six friends to Chongqing Temple to see the peonies in bloom. Strolling in the west corridor, they composed poems together. A close friend of Li's named Wei Xiaqing, a native of Chang'an, was one of the party. "Spring is beautiful and flowers are in bloom," he told Li. "But your old love nurses her grief in her lonely room. It is really cruel of you to

abandon her.   A true man would not do this.   Think
it over again!"

As Wei was sighing and reproaching Li, up came a
young gallant wearing a yellow silk shirt and carrying
a crossbow.

He was handsome and splendidly dressed, but attended only by a Central Asian boy with cropped hair.
Walking behind them, he overheard their conversation; and presently he stepped forward and bowed to Li,
saying, "Is your name not Li? My family comes from the
east, and we are related to the royal house. Though I
have no literary talent myself, I value it in others.   I
have long been an admirer of yours and hoped to make
your acquaintance, and today I am lucky enough to
meet you. My humble house is not far from here, and
I have musicians to entertain you.   I have eight or nine
beautiful girls too, and a dozen good horses, all of them
at your disposal.   I only hope you will honour me with
a visit."

When Li's friends heard this, they were delighted.
They rode along after this young gallant, who swiftly
turned corner after corner until they reached the Shengye
quarter. Since they were approaching Jade's house, Li
was reluctant to go any farther and made some excuse
to turn back.

But the stranger said: "My humble home is only a
stone's throw from here. Don't leave us now!" He took
hold of Li's bridle and pulled his horse along.

In a moment they had reached the girl's house.   Li
was dismayed and tried to turn back, but the other
quickly ordered attendants to help him dismount and
lead him inside. They pushed him through the gate
and bolted it, calling out, "Master Li is here!" Then

exclamations of joy and surprise could be heard from the whole house.

The night before, Jade had dreamed that Li was brought to her bedside by a man in a yellow shirt and that she was told to take off her shoes. When she woke up she told her mother this dream, and said, "Shoes symbolize union. That means that husband and wife will meet again. But to take them off means separation. We shall be united then parted again — for ever. Judging by this dream, I shall see him once more and after that I shall die."

In the morning she asked her mother to dress her hair for her. Her mother thought she was raving and paid no attention, but when Jade insisted she consented. And no sooner was her hair done than Li arrived.

Jade had been ill so long that she could not even turn in bed without help. But on hearing that her lover had come she got up swiftly, changed her clothes and hurried out like one possessed. Confronting Li in silence, she fixed angry eyes on him. So frail she could hardly stand, she kept averting her face and then, against her will, looking back, till all present were moved to tears.

Soon several dozen dishes of food and wine were brought in. And when the company asked in astonishment where this feast had come from, they found it had been ordered by the young gallant. The table spread, they sat down. Jade, though she had turned away from Li, kept stealing long glances at him; and finally raising her cup of wine, she poured a libation on the ground and said, "I am the unhappiest of women, and you are the most heartless of men. Dying young of a broken heart, I shall not be able to look after my mother; and I must bid farewell for ever to my silk dresses and music, to suffer torments in hell. This is your doing, sir! Farewell! After death I shall become an avenging spirit and give your wives and concubines no peace."

Grasping Li's arm with her left hand, she threw her cup to the ground. Then, after crying out several times, she fell dead. Her mother placed her body on Li's knee and told him to call her, but he could not revive her.

Li put on mourning and wept bitterly during the wake. The night before the obsequies she appeared to him within the funeral curtain, as beautiful as in life. She was wearing a pomegranate-red skirt, purple tunic, and red and green cape. Leaning against the curtain and fingering the embroidered tassels, she looked at him and said, "You must still have some feeling for me, to see me off. That is a comfort to me here among the shades." With that she vanished. The next day she was buried at Yusuyuan near the capital. After mourning by her grave, Li went back; and a month later he married his cousin. But he was in low spirits after all that had happened.

In the fifth month, Li went with his wife to his post at Zheng County. About ten days after their arrival, he was sleeping with his wife when he heard soft hoots outside the curtain, and looking out he saw a very handsome young man hiding behind the hangings and beckoning repeatedly to his wife. Li leaped up in agitation and went round the curtain several times to look for the intruder, but no one was there. This made him so suspicious that he gave his wife no peace until some friends persuaded him to make it up and he began to feel a little better. About ten days later, however, he came home to find his wife playing her lute on the couch, when an engraved rhinoceros-horn case, little over an inch in diameter and tied with a flimsy silk love-knot, was thrown into the room. This case fell on his wife's lap. When Li opened it, he found two love-peas, one Spanish fly as well as other aphrodisiacs and love-charms. Howling like a wild beast in his anger, he seized the lute and beat his wife with it as he demanded the truth. But she could not clear herself. After that he often beat her savagely and treated her with great cruelty; and finally he denounced her in the court and divorced her.

After Li divorced his wife, he soon became suspicious of the maidservants and women slaves whom he had favoured, and some he even killed in his jealousy. Once he went to Yangzhou and bought a famous courtesan named Ying, who was the eleventh child of her family. She was so charming and beautiful that Li was very fond of her. But when they were together he liked to tell her about another girl he had purchased, and how he had punished her for various faults. He told her such things every day to make her fear him, so that she would not dare to take other lovers. Whenever he went out, he would leave her on the bed covered up with a bath-tub which was sealed all round; and upon his return he would examine the tub carefully before letting her out. He also kept a very sharp dagger and would say to his maids, "This is Gexi steel. It's good for cutting the throats of unfaithful women!"

Whatever women he had, he would soon grow suspicious of them, and he was a jealous husband to the two other wives he married later.

Governor of the Southern Tributary State

Li Gongzuo

CHUNYU Fen, a native of Dongping and a well-known gallant of the Yangtse River region, was fond of drinking, hot-tempered and recklessly indifferent to conventions. He had amassed great wealth and acted as patron to many dashing young men. Because of his military prowess he had been made an adjutant of the Huainan Army, but in a fit of drunkenness he offended his general and was dismissed. Then in his disappointment he let himself go and gave his days to drinking.

Chunyu's home was some three miles east of Yangzhou. South of his house there was a huge old ash tree with great branches, thick with foliage, which shaded an acre of land; and under this tree Chunyu and his boon companions drank daily to their hearts' content. In the ninth month of the tenth year of the Zhen Yuan period (AD 794), Chunyu got drunk, and two of his friends carried him home and laid him in the eastern chamber. "You had better have a sleep," they said, "while we give the horses some fodder and wash our feet. We shan't go until you feel better."

Li Gongzuo (c. 770-850) was a friend of the writer Bai Xingjian. Three other stories by him are extant.

He took off his cap and rested his head on the pillow, lying there in a tipsy state, half dreaming and half awake. Presently he saw two messengers in purple, who entered to kneel before him and announce, "His Majesty the king of Ashendon has sent us, his humble subjects, to invite you to his kingdom."

Chunyu arose from his couch, dressed himself and followed the messengers to the gate, where he found a small green carriage drawn by four horses. Seven or eight attendants standing there helped him into this. Driving out of the gate, they made for the ash tree and — to Chunyu's amazement — headed down the hollow under the tree. However, he dared ask no questions. The scenery along the road — the mountains and rivers, trees and plants — looked different from the world of men. The climate too had changed. After they had travelled about ten miles, city walls came into sight, and the highway began to be thronged with carriages and people. The footmen on the carriage kept calling out to clear the road and the pedestrians moved hurriedly out of their way. They entered a great city through a turreted red gate over which was inscribed in letters of gold "The Great Kingdom of Ashendon". The gate-keepers bestirred themselves and bowed low to them.

Then a rider cantered up, calling, "As His Highness the prince consort has travelled so far, His Majesty orders him to be taken to the East Hostel to rest." And he led the way.

Chunyu saw a gate in front swing open, and alighting from the carriage he passed through it. Here were brightly painted and finely carved balustrades and pilasters among terraces of blossoming trees and rare fruits, while tables and rugs, cushions and screens had been set ready in the hall where a rich feast was laid out. Chunyu was enchanted. Presently it was anounced that the prime minister had arrived, and Chunyu went to the foot of the hall steps to await him respectfully. Dressed in purple and holding an ivory sceptre, the minister approached, and they paid their respects to each other. This done, the minister said, "Though our land is far from yours, our king has invited you here because he hopes for an alliance with you by marriage."

"How can a humble person like myself aspire so high?" replied the young man.

The minister asked Chunyu to follow him to the palace. They walked a hundred yards and entered a red gate where spears, axes, and halberds were displayed and among several hundred officers who stood by the side of the road to make way for them was Chunyu's old drinking friend Zhou. Chunyu was secretly delighted, but dared not go forward to accost him.

Then the minister led Chunyu up to a court where guards were standing solemnly in formation, showing that they were in the royal presence. He saw a tall, imposing figure on the throne, wearing a white silk robe and a bright red cap. Overcome by awe, he did not look up, but bowed as he was directed by the attendants. "At your father's wish," said the king, "we have asked you to our unworthy kingdom to offer you our second daughter as your wife." When Chunyu kept his head lowered and dared not reply, the king told him, "You may go back to the guest house and prepare for the ceremony."

As the minister accompanied him back, Chunyu was thinking hard. Since his father was a frontier general who had been reported missing, it was possible that, having made peace with the border kingdoms, he was responsible for this invitation. Still the young man was bewildered and at a loss to account for it.

That evening, amid pomp and splendour, betrothal gifts of lambs, swans and silk were displayed. There was music of stringed and bamboo instruments, feasting by the light of lanterns and candles, and a concourse of carriages and horsemen. Some of the girls present were addressed as the nymphs of Huayang or Qingxi, others as the fairies of the upper or lower region. Attended by a large retinue, they wore green phoenix head-dresses, gold cloud-like garments and golden trinkets and precious stones that dazzled the eye. These girls frolicked and played charming tricks on Chunyu who found it hard to answer their clever repartee.

"On the last Spring Purification Festival,"* one girl said, "I went with Lady Lingzhi to Chanzhi Monastery to watch Youyan perform the Brahmana dance in the Indian Quadrangle. I was sitting with the girls on the stone bench on the north side when you and your young gallants arrived, and got off your horses to watch. You accosted us and teased us and made jokes — don't you remember how Qiongying and I tied a scarlet scarf on the bamboo? Then, on the sixteenth of the seventh month, I went with Shang Zhenzi to Xiaogan Monastery to listen to Monk Qi Xuan discoursing on the Avalokiteshvara sutra. I donated two gold phoenix-shaped hair-pins and my friend one rhinoceros-horn case. You

---

* On this festival, which falls on the third day of the third month, people used to bathe in the rivers to "purify" themselves and so guard against evil during the coming year.

were there too, and asked the monk to let you see them. After admiring them and praising the workmanship at some length, you turned to us and said, 'These pretty things and their owners surely can't belong to the world of men!' Then you asked my name and wanted to know where I lived, but I wouldn't tell you. You kept staring at me as if you were quite lovelorn — don't you remember?"

Chunyu replied by quoting the song:

> Deep in my heart it is hidden,
> How can I ever forget?

And the girls said, "Who could imagine that you would become our relative?"

Just then up came three men in magnificent clothes. Bowing to Chunyu, they declared, "By His Majesty's order we have come to be your groomsmen." One of them looked like an old friend.

"Aren't you Tian Zihua of Fengyi?" Chunyu asked him. When the other said that he was, Chunyu stepped forward to grasp his hand and they talked about the past.

Asked how he came to be there, Tian replied, "On my travels I met Lord Duan, the prime minister, and he became my patron." When Chunyu inquired if he knew of Zhou's presence there, he answered, "Zhou has done very well. He is now the city commandant and has great influence. On several occasions he has done me a favour."

They talked cheerfully until it was announced that the prince consort should go to the wedding. As the three groomsmen handed him his sword, pendants, robes and head-dress and helped him put them on, Tian said, "I never thought to attend such a grand ceremony for you today. You mustn't forget your old friends."

Several dozen fairy maids now began to play rare music, piercingly tender and infinitely sad, the like of which Chunyu had never heard before. Dozens of other attendants held candles all the way down a mile-long path lined on both sides with gold and emerald-green screens vividly painted and intricately carved. He sat up straight in the carriage, rather nervous, while Tian joked to put him at his ease. The girls he had seen were arriving too in phoenix-winged carriages. When he reached the gate of Xiuyi Palace, the girls were there too, and Chunyu was asked to alight. He went through a ceremony just like that in the world of men, at the end of which screens and fans were removed, enabling him to see his bride, the Princess of the Golden Bough. She was about fifteen, lovely as a goddess and well trained in the marriage ceremony.

After the wedding Chunyu and the princess came to love each other dearly, and his power and prestige increased daily. His equipage and entertainments were second only to the king's. One day the king took him and some other officials as his guards to hunt on the Divine Tortoise Mountain in the west, where there were high peaks, wide marshlands and luxuriant forests stocked with all kinds of birds and beasts. The hunters came back with a big bag of game that evening.

Another day Chunyu said to the king, "On my wedding day Your Majesty told me you had sent for me in compliance with my father's wishes. My father served formerly as a general at the frontier. After a defeat he was reported missing, and I have had no news of him for eighteen years. Since Your Majesty knows where he is now, I would like to call on him."

"Your father is still serving at the northern frontier," replied the king quickly. "We are in constant touch. You had better just write to him. There is no need for you to go there." The king ordered the princess to prepare gifts to send to her father-in-law, and after a few days a reply came in his handwriting. He expressed his longing for his son and wrote just as in former letters, asking whether certain relatives were still alive and what news there was of their home-town. Since the distance between them was so great, he said, it was difficult to send news. His letter was sad and full of grief. He told Chunyu not to come, but promised that they would meet in three years' time. With this letter in his hands, Chunyu wept bitterly, unable to restrain himself.

One day the princess asked him, "Don't you ever want to take up an official post?"

"I am used to a carefree life," he answered. "I don't understand official work."

"Just take a post," she said, "and I will help you." Then she spoke to the king.

A few days later the king said, "All is not well in my southern tributary state, and the governor has been dismissed. I would like to use your talents to set their affairs in order. You might go there with my daughter." When Chunyu consented, the king ordered those in charge to get his baggage ready. Gold, jade and silk, cases and servants, carriages and horsemen formed a long baggage train when he and the princess were ready to leave. And since Chunyu had mixed with gallants as a young man and never dreamed of becoming an official, he found this most gratifying.

He sent a memorandum to the king, saying, "As the son of a military family, I have never studied the art of government. Now that I have been given this important post, I fear I shall not only disgrace myself but ruin the prestige of the court. I would therefore like to seek far and wide for wise and talented men to help me. I have noticed that City Commandant Zhou of Yingchuan is a loyal, honest officer, who firmly upholds the law and would make a good minister. Then there is Tian Zihua, a gentleman of Fengyi, who is prudent and full of stratagems and has probed deeply into the principles of government. I have known both these men for ten years. I understand their talents and consider them trustworthy, and therefore I ask to have Zhou appointed the chief councillor and Tian the minister of finance of my state. For then the government will be well administered and the laws well kept." The two men were then appointed to these posts by the king.

The evening of Chunyu's departure, the king and queen gave a farewell feast for him south of the capital.

"The southern state is a great province," said the king. "The land is rich and the people prosperous, and you must adopt a benevolent policy there. With Zhou and Tian assisting you, I hope you will do well and come up to our expectations."

Meantime the queen told the princess, "Your husband is impetuous and fond of drinking, and he is still young. A wife should be gentle and obedient. I trust you to look after him well. Though you will not be too far from us, you will no longer be able to greet us every

morning and evening, and I find it hard not to shed
tears now that you are going away." Then Chunyu and
the princess bowed, got into their carriage and started
south. They talked cheerfully on the way, and several
days later reached their destination.

The officials of the province, the monks and priests,
elders, musicians, attendants and guards had all come
out in welcome. The streets were thronged, while
drums and bells could be heard for miles around.
Chunyu saw a goodly array of turrets and pavilions as
he entered the great city gate, above which was inscribed
in letters of gold "The Southern Tributary State". In
front there were red windows and a large gate with a
fine view into the distance. After his arrival he studied
the local conditions and helped all who were sick or
distressed, entrusting his government to Zhou and Tian,
who administered the province well. He remained
governor there for twenty years, and the people
benefiting from his good rule sang his praises and
set up tablets extolling his virtue or built temples to
him. As a result, the king honoured him even more:
he was given fiefs and titles and exalted to the position of a grand councillor of state, while both Zhou and
Tian also became well-known as good officials, and
were promoted several times. Chunyu had five sons
and two daughters. His sons were given official posts
reserved for the nobility, while his daughters were married into the royal family. Thus his fame and renown
were unrivalled.

One year the kingdom of Sandalvine attacked this
province, and the king ordered Chunyu to raise an army
to defend it. Chunyu made Zhou commander of thirty
thousand troops to resist the invaders at Jade Tower

City, but Zhou proved proud and reckless, under-estimating the enemy. His troops were routed and, abandoning his armour, he fled back alone to the provincial capital at night. Meanwhile the invaders, after capturing their baggage train and arms, had with-drawn. Chunyu had Zhou arrested and asked to be punished, but the king pardoned them both.

That same month Zhou developed a boil on his back and died. Ten days later the princess died of illness too, and Chunyu's request to leave the province and ac-company the hearse to the capital was granted. Tian, the minister of finance, was appointed deputy in his place. Bowed down with grief, Chunyu followed the hearse. On the way many people wept, officers and common citizens paid their last homage, while great crowds blocked the way and clung to the carriage. When he reached Ashendon, the king and queen were waiting outside the capital, wearing mourning and weeping. The princess was posthumously entitled Shun Yi (Obedient and Graceful). Guards, canopies and musi-cians were provided, and she was buried at Coiling Dragon Mount some three miles east of the city. During the same month, Zhou's son Rongxin also arrived with his father's hearse.

Now though Chunyu had been ruling over a tributary state outside the kingdom for many years, he had man-aged to keep on good terms with all the nobles and influential officers at court. After his return to the cap-ital he behaved unconventionally and gathered around himself many associates and followers, his power grow-ing so rapidly that the king began to suspect him. Then some citizens reported to the king that a mysterious portent had appeared and the state was doomed to suffer a great catastrophe: the capital would be removed and the ancestral temples destroyed. This would be caused by some man of foreign birth who was close to the royal family. After deliberation the ministers decided that there was danger in Chunyu's luxury and presumption; accordingly the king deprived him of his attendants and forbade him to have any further dealings with his associates, ordering him to live in retirement.

Conscious that he had not governed badly all these years in his province, but was being slandered, Chunyu was in low spirits. The king, sensing this, said to him, "You have been my son-in-law for more than twenty years. Unhappily my daughter died young and could not live with you till old age. This is a great misfortune." Then the queen took charge of his children herself, and the king said, "You have left your home for a long time. You had better go back now for a while to see your relatives. Leave your children here and do not worry about them. In three years we shall fetch you back."

"Isn't this my home?" asked Chunyu. "What other home have I to go back to?"

"You came from the world of men," replied the king with a laugh. "This is not your home." At first Chunyu felt as if he were dreaming, but then he remembered how he had come there and, shedding tears, asked for permission to return. The king ordered his attendants to see him off, and with a bow Chunyu took his leave.

The same two messengers dressed in purple accompanied him out of the gate. But there he was shocked to see a shabby carriage with no attendants or envoys to accompany him. He got into the carriage, however, and after driving some miles they left the city behind. They travelled the same way that he had first come by.

The mountains, rivers and plains were unchanged, but the two messengers with Chunyu looked so seedy that he felt let down. When he asked them when they would reach Yangzhou, they went on singing without paying any attention. Only when he insisted did they answer, "Soon."

Presently they emerged from the hollow and Chunyu saw his own village unchanged. Sadness seized him, and he could not help shedding tears. The two messengers helped him down from the carriage, through the door of his house and up the steps. Then he saw himself lying in the eastern chamber, and was so frightened that he dared not approach. At that the two messengers called his name aloud several times, and he woke up.

He saw his servants sweeping the courtyard. His two guests were still washing their feet by the couch, the slanting sun had not yet set behind the west wall and his unfinished wine was still by the east window — but he had lived through a whole generation in his dream! Deeply moved, he could not help sighing. And when he called his two friends and told them, they were equally amazed. They went out to look for the hollow under the ash tree, and Chunyu, pointing to it, said, "This is where I went in the dream."

His friends believed this must be the work of some fox fairy or tree spirit, so servants were ordered to fetch an axe and cut through the tree trunk and branches to find where the hollow ended. It was some ten feet long, terminating in a cavity lit by the sun and large enough to hold a couch. In this were mounds of earth which resembled city walls, pavilions and courts, and swarms of ants were gathered there. In the ant-hill was a small, reddish tower occupied by two huge ants, three

inches long, with white wings and red heads. They
were surrounded by a few dozen big ants, and other
ants dared not approach them. These huge ants were the
king and queen, and this was the capital of Ashendon.

Then the men followed up another hole which lay
under the southern branch of the tree and was at least
forty feet long. In this tunnel there was another ant-
hill with small towers, which swarmed with ants. This
was the southern tributary state which Chunyu had
governed. Another large, rambling tunnel of a fantastic
shape ran westwards for twenty feet, and in this they
found a rotten tortoise shell as big as a peck measure,
soaked by rain and covered by luxuriant grass. This
was the Divine Tortoise Mountain, where Chunyu had
hunted. They followed up yet another tunnel more
than ten feet long in the east, where the gnarled roots
of the tree had twisted into the shape of a dragon. Here
there was a small earthen mound about a foot high,
and this was the grave of the princess, Chunyu's wife.

As he thought back, Chunyu was very shaken, for all
that they had discovered coincided with his dream. He
would not let his friends destroy these ant-hills, and
ordered that the tunnels be covered up as before. That
night, however, there was a sudden storm, and the next
morning when he examined the holes the ants had gone.
Thus the prophecy that Ashendon would suffer a great
catastrophe and that the capital would be removed was
realized. Then he thought of the invasion by the kingdom of Sandalvine, and asked his two friends to trace
it. They found that some six hundred yards east of his
house was a river-bed long since dry, and next to it
grew a big sandal tree so thickly covered with vines
that the sun could not shine through it. A small hole

beside it, where a swarm of ants had gathered, must be the kingdom of Sandalvine.

If even the mysteries of ants are so unfathomable, what then of the changes caused by big beasts in the hills and woods?

At that time Chunyu's friends Zhou and Tian were both in Liuhe County, and he had not seen them for ten days. He sent a servant posthaste to make inquiries, and found that Zhou had died of a sudden illness, while Tian was lying ill in bed. Then Chunyu realized how empty his dream had been, and that all was vanity too in the world of men. He therefore became a Taoist and abstained from wine and women. Three years later he died at home, in his forty-seventh year, just as predicted in the dream.

In the eighth month of the eleventh year of the Zhen Yuan period (AD 795), while on a journey from Suzhou to Luoyang I had stopped at Huaipu and met Chunyu by chance. I questioned him and looked at the ant-hills, going into his story very thoroughly. Believing it to be quite genuine, I have written this tale for those who may be interested. Although it deals with supernatural and unorthodox things, it may have a moral for the ambitious. Let future readers not think this narrative a mere series of coincidences, and let them beware of taking pride in worldly fame and position!

For, as Li Zhao, former adjutant general of Huazhou commented:

> *His reputation reaches to the skies,*
> *His influence can make a kingdom fall,*
> *And yet this pomp and power, after all,*
> *Are but an ant-heap in the wise man's eyes.*

Story of a Singsong Girl

Bai Xingjian

IN the Tian Bao period (742-756) the Lord of Ying-yang, whose name and surname I will omit, was Governor of Changzhou. He was highly respected and extremely rich. When our story starts he was fifty and had a son of nearly twenty — an intelligent lad of outstanding literary ability, the admiration of all his contemporaries. His father loved him dearly and had high hopes of him. "This," he would say, "is the 'thousand-league colt' of our family." When the time came for the lad to take the provincial examination, his father gave him fine clothes and equipage for the journey, and money for his expenses in the capital. "With your gifts you should succeed at the first attempt," he said. "But I am giving you an allowance for two years, and a generous one at that, to enable you to work without worrying." The young man was quite confident too, and saw himself passing the examination as clearly as he saw the palm of his own hand.

Setting out from Changzhou he reached the capital in little more than a month and took a house in the Bu-zheng quarter. One day on his way back from the East

---

Bai Xingjian (776-826) was the brother of the famous poet Bai Juyi. His other works include the story *The Three Dreams.*

Market, he entered the eastern gate of the Pingkang quarter to visit a friend who lived in the southwest part. When he reached Mingke Lane, he saw a house with a rather narrow gate and courtyard. The house itself, however, was a grand one, and from the gate you could see many buildings stretching back. One half of the double door was open and at it stood a girl, attended by her young maid. She was of an exquisite, bewitching beauty, such as the world had seldom seen.

When he saw her, the young man unconsciously reined in his horse and hesitated, unable to tear himself away. He deliberately dropped his whip and waited for his servant to pick it up, all the time staring at the girl. She, for her part, returned his gaze with a look of answering admiration. But in the end he went away without daring to speak to her.

After that he was like a man distracted, and secretly begged a friend who knew the capital well to find out who she was.

"The house belongs to a courtesan named Li," his friend told him.

"Is it possible to get her?" he asked.

"She is very well off," said his friend, "because her previous dealings have been with rich and aristocratic families, who paid her lavishly. Unless you spend a million cash, she will have nothing to do with you."

"All I want is to win her," answered the young man. "I don't mind if she costs a million."

Some days later he put on his best clothes and set out, with a train of attendants behind him, for her house. When he knocked at the door, a young maid opened it.

"Can you tell me whose house this is?" the young man asked.

The maid did not answer, but ran back into the house calling out at the top of her voice: "Here's the gentleman who dropped his whip the other day!"

The girl replied with evident pleasure: "Ask him in. I'll come as soon as I've changed my clothes and tidied myself."

The young man hearing this was inwardly overjoyed as he followed the maid into the house. He saw the girl's mother — a grey-haired woman with a bent back — and bowing low said to her: "I hear that you have a vacant courtyard which you might be willing to let. Is that true?"

"I am afraid it is too shabby and small for a gentleman like you," she said. "You may take it if you like, but I wouldn't dare ask for any rent." She then took him into the reception room, which was a very splendid one, and asked him to be seated, saying: "I have a daughter who is very young and has few accomplishments, but who enjoys the company of visitors. I should like you to meet her."

With that she called for her daughter. The girl had sparkling eyes and dazzling white arms, and moved with such consummate grace that the young man could only leap to his feet in confusion and did not dare raise his eyes. When they had greeted each other, he made a few remarks about the weather, conscious as he did so that her beauty was such as he had never seen before.

They sat down again. Tea was made and wine poured out. The vessels used were spotlessly clean. He stayed on until it was late and the curfew drum could be heard all around, when the old lady asked if he lived far away.

He answered untruthfully: "Several miles beyond

Yanping Gate," hoping that they would ask him to stay.

"The drum has sounded," she said. "You will have to leave at once, if you don't want to break the law."

"I was enjoying myself so much," said the young man, "that I didn't notice how late it was. My house is a long way off, and I have no relations in the city. What am I to do?"

"If you don't think our house too shabby," put in the girl, "what harm would there be in your spending the night here?"

He glanced several times at the old lady, who assented.

Calling his servants, he ordered them to bring two bolts of silk* which he offered for the expenses of a feast. But the girl stopped him and protested laughingly: "No, you are our guest. We would like to entertain you tonight with our humble household's rough and ready fare. You can treat us another time." He tried to refuse, but in the end she had her way, and they all moved to the western hall. The curtains, screens, blinds and couches were of dazzling splendour, the toilet-boxes, coverlets and pillows the height of luxury. Candles were lighted and an excellent meal was served.

After supper, when the old lady had retired, the young man and girl began to talk intimately, laughing and joking completely at their ease.

"I passed your house the other day," said the young man, "and you happened to be standing at the door. After that, I couldn't get you out of my head. Lying

---

* In the Tang dynasty silk was often used as money.

down to rest or sitting down to eat, I couldn't stop thinking of you."

"It was just the same with me," she answered.

"You know, I didn't come today simply to look for lodgings," he said. "I came hoping you would grant the wish of my life. But I wasn't sure what my fate would be. . . ."

As he was speaking the old woman came back and asked what they were saying. Upon being told, she laughed and said: " 'There is a natural attraction between the sexes.' When lovers are agreed, not even their parents can control them. But my daughter is of humble birth — are you sure she is fit to share your bed?"

The young man immediately came down from the dais and, bowing low, said: "Please accept me as your servant!" After that the old lady regarded him as her son-in-law; they drank heavily together and finally parted. Next morning he had all his baggage brought round to their house and made it his home.

Henceforward he shut himself up there, and his friends heard no more of him. He mixed only with actors, dancers and people of that kind, passing the time in wild sports and aimless feasting. When his money was spent he sold his horses and men-servants. In little over a year all his money, property, attendants and horses were gone.

The old lady had begun to treat him coldly, but the girl seemed more devoted to him than ever. One day she said to him: "We have been together a year, but I am still not with child. They say that the spirit of the Bamboo Grove answers prayers as surely as an echo. Shall we go to his temple and offer a libation?"

Not suspecting any plot, the young man was delighted. And having pawned his coat to buy wine and sacrificial meat, he went with her to the temple and prayed to the spirit. They spent two nights there and started back the third day, the young man riding a donkey behind the girl's carriage. When they reached the north gate of the Xuanyang quarter, she turned to him and said: "My aunt's house is in a lane to the east near here. Suppose we rest there for a little?"

He fell in with her wishes, and they had not gone more than a hundred paces when he saw a wide drive and their servant stopped the carriage, saying: "We have arrived." The young man got down and was met by a man-servant who came out to ask who they were. When told that it was Mistress Li, he went back and announced her. Presently a woman of about forty came out.

She greeted our hero and asked: "Has my niece arrived?" The girl alighted from the carriage and her aunt welcomed her, saying: "Why haven't you been here for so long?" They exchanged glances and laughed. Then the girl introduced him to her aunt, after which they all went into a side garden near the western gate. There was a pavilion set in a profusion of bamboos and trees amid quiet pools and summer-houses.

"Does this garden belong to your aunt?" the young man asked.

The girl laughed, but instead of answering she spoke of something else.

Delicious tea and cakes were served. But almost at once a man galloped up on a Fergana horse which was all in a lather. "The old lady has been taken very ill," he gasped. "She is beginning to be delirious. You had better hurry back."

"I am so worried," said the girl to her aunt. "Let me take the horse and ride on ahead. Then I will send it back, and you and my husband can come along later." The young man was anxious to go with her, but the aunt whispered to her maid to stop him at the gate.

"My sister must be dead by now," she said. "You and I ought to discuss the funeral together. What good can you do by running after her in an emergency like this?" So he stayed, to discuss the funeral and mourning rites.

It grew late, but still the horse had not come back. "I wonder what can have happened?" said the aunt. "You had better hurry over to see. I will come on later."

The young man set out. When he reached the house he found the gate firmly locked and sealed. Astounded, he questioned the neighbours. "Mistress Li only rented this house," they told him. "When her lease was up, the landlord took it back, and she moved away. She left two days ago." But when he asked her new address, they did not know it.

He thought of hurrying back to the Xuanyang quarter to question the aunt, but it was already too late. So he pawned some of his clothes to procure himself supper and a bed. He was too angry to sleep, however, and did not close his eyes from dusk till dawn. Early in the morning he rode on his donkey to the aunt's house, but although he knocked on the door for the time it takes for a meal, no one answered. At last his loud shouts brought a footman slowly to the door. The young man immediately asked for the aunt.

"She doesn't live here," answered the footman.

"But she was here yesterday evening," the young man protested. "Are you trying to fool me?" He inquired whose house it was.

"This is the residence of His Excellency Master Cui. Yesterday somebody hired his courtyard to entertain a cousin coming from a distance, but they were gone before nightfall."

Bewildered and nearly distracted, the young man did not know what to do. He went back to his old lodgings in the Buzheng quarter. The landlord was sorry for him and offered to feed him; but in his despair he could eat nothing, and after three days he fell seriously ill. In another fortnight he was so weak that the landlord feared he could not live, and carried him to the undertakers. As he lay there at the point of death, all the undertakers in the market pitied him and nursed him, until he was well enough to walk with a stick.

The undertakers then hired him by the day to hold up the mourning curtains, and in this way he earned just enough to support himself. In a few months he grew quite strong again, but the mourners' chants always made him regret that he could not change places with the dead, and he would burst out sobbing and weeping, unable to restrain his tears. When he went home he would imitate their chants. Being a man of intelligence, he very soon mastered the art and became the most expert mourner in the whole captial.

It happened that the undertakers in the East and West Markets at this time were rivals. The undertakers in the East Market turned out magnificent hearses and biers — in this respect they were unrivalled — but the mourners they provided were rather poor. Hearing of

our hero's skill, the chief undertaker offered him twenty
thousand cash for his services; and the experts of the
East Market secretly taught the young man all the
fresh tunes they knew, singing in harmony with him.
This went on in secret for several weeks. Then the two
chief undertakers agreed to give an exhibition in Tian-
men Street to see which was the better. The loser would
forfeit 50,000 cash to cover the cost of the refreshments
provided. An agreement to this effect was drawn up and
duly witnessed.

Tens of thousands of people gathered to watch the
contest. The chief of the quarter got wind of the proceed-
ings and told the chief of police. The chief of police
told the city magistrate. Very soon all the citizens
of the capital were hurrying to the spot and every house
in the city was empty.

The exhibition started at dawn. Coaches, hearses, and
all kinds of funeral trappings had been displayed for a
whole morning, but still the undertakers from the West
Market could establish no superiority, and their chief
was filled with shame.   He built a platform in the south
corner of the square, and a man with a long beard came
forward, holding a hand-bell and attended by several
assistants. He wagged his beard, raised his eyebrows,
folded his arms and bowed. Then, mounting the platform, he sang the *White Horse* dirge. Proud of his skill,
he looked to right and to left as if he knew himself
unrivalled.   Shouts of approval were heard on every
side, and he was convinced that he must be the best
dirge singer of his time who could not possibly be surpassed.

Presently the chief undertaker of the East Market
built a platform in the north corner of the square, and

a young man in a black cap came forward, accompanied by five or six assistants and carrying a bunch of hearse-plumes in his hand. This was our hero.

He adjusted his clothes, looked slowly up and down, then cleared his throat and began to sing with an air of diffidence. He sang the dirge *Dew on the Garlic*, and his voice rose so shrill and clear that its echoes shook the forest trees. Before he had finished the first verse, all who heard were sobbing and hiding their tears. They started jeering at the chief undertaker of the West Market until, overcome by shame, he stealthily put down the money he had forfeited and fled, to the amazement of the crowd.

Now the emperor had recently ordered the governors of outlying provinces to confer with him at the capital once a year. This was called the "Yearly Reckoning". Thus our hero's father happened to be at the capital too, and he and some of his colleagues, discarding their official robes and insignia, had slipped out to watch the contest. With them was an old servant, the husband of the young man's foster-nurse. Recognizing our hero's accent and gait, he wanted to accost him but dared not and wept. Surprised, the Lord of Yingyang asked him why he was crying.

"Sir," replied the servant, "the young man who is singing reminds me of your lost son."

"My son was murdered by robbers because I gave him too much money," said the Lord of Yingyang. "This cannot be he." So saying, he began to weep too and went back to his lodging.

The old servant then went again to ask some of the undertakers: "Who was that singer? Where did he learn such skill?" They told him it was the son of such a one, and when he asked the young man's own name, that too was unfamiliar. The old servant was so much puzzled that he determined to put the matter to the test for himself. But when the young man saw him he gave a start, and tried to hide in the crowd. The servant caught hold of his sleeve, and said: "Surely it is you!" Then they embraced and wept, and presently went back together.

But when the young man came to his father's lodging, the Lord of Yingyang was angry with him and said: "Your conduct has disgraced the family. How dare you show your face again?" So saying he took him out of the house and led him to the ground between Qujiang and Xingyuan. Here he stripped him naked and gave him several hundred strokes with his horsewhip, till the young man succumbed to the pain and collapsed. Then his father left, thinking he was dead.

However, the young man's singing-master had asked some of his friends to keep a secret watch on him, and now they came back and told the others what had happened. They were all greatly upset, and two men were dispatched with a reed mat to bury him. When they got there they found his heart still warm, and when they had held him up for some time he started breathing again. So they carried him home and gave him liquid food through a reed pipe. The next morning he recovered consciousness, but for a whole month he was unable to move his hands and feet. Moreover, the sores left by the thrashing festered and gave out such a stench that his friends could not stand it, and one night they abandoned him by the roadside.

The passers-by, however, took pity on him and threw him scraps of food, so that he did not starve. After

three months he was well enough to hobble about with
a stick. Clad in a linen coat — which was knotted together in a hundred places, so that it looked as tattered
as a quail's tail — and carrying a broken saucer in his
hand, he started to beg his way through the various
quarters of the city. Autumn had now turned to winter.
He spent his nights in lavatories and caves and his
days haunting the markets and booths.

One day when it was snowing hard, hunger and cold
had driven him into the streets. His bitter cry pierced
all who heard it to the heart. But the snow was so
heavy that hardly a house had its outer door open.

When he reached the eastern gate of the Anyi quarter,
he went north along the wall until he came to the seventh
or eighth house which he found had the left half of its
double door open. This was the house where the girl
Li was then living, although the young man did not
know it.

He stood at the door wailing persistently. And
hunger and cold had made his cry so pitiful that you
could scarcely bear to hear it.

The girl heard it from her room, and said to her
maid: "That is my lover. I know his voice." She flew
to the door and found him there, so emaciated and
covered with sores that he seemed scarcely human.

"Can it be you?" she exclaimed, deeply moved. The
young man simply nodded, too overcome by anger and
excitement to speak.

She threw her arms round his neck, then wrapped
him in her own embroidered jacket, led him to the
western chamber and said in a choked voice: "It is all
my fault that this has happened to you." And with these
words she swooned.

The old woman came hurrying over in great alarm, crying: "What is it?" When the girl told her who had come, she immediately raised objections. "Send him packing!" she cried. "What did you bring him in here for?"

But the girl looked grave and protested: "No! This is the son of a noble house. Once he rode in grand carriages and wore fine clothes. But within a year of coming to our house he lost all he had. And then we got rid of him by a contemptible trick. We have ruined his career and made him despised by his fellow men. The love of father and son is implanted by Heaven; yet because of us his father hardened his heart and tried to kill him, then abandoned him so that he was reduced to this state.

"Everyone in the land knows that it was I who brought him to this. The court is full of his relatives. Once the authorities come to investigate this business, we shall be ruined. And since we have deceived Heaven and injured men, no spirits will take our part. Do we want to offend the gods and bring such misfortune on ourselves?

"I have lived as your daughter for twenty years, and my earnings amount to nearly a thousand pieces of gold. You are over sixty now, and I would like to give you enough to cover your expenses for another twenty years to buy my freedom, so that I can live somewhere else with this young man. We will not go far away. I shall see to it that we are near enough to pay our respects to you both morning and evening."

The old woman saw that the girl's mind was made up, so she gave her consent. When she had paid her ransom, the girl had several hundred pieces of gold left, and with them she hired a few rooms, five doors to the north. Here she gave the young man a bath, changed his clothes, fed him first with hot gruel, which was easy to digest, and later on with cheese and milk.

In a few weeks she was giving him all the choicest delicacies of land and sea. She clothed him, too, in the finest caps, shoes and stockings she could buy. In a few months he began to put on weight, and by the end of the year his health was as good as ever.

One day the girl said to him: "Now you are strong again and have got back your nerve. Try to think how much you remember of your old literary studies."

After a moment's thought he answered: "About a quarter."

Then she ordered her carriage to be got ready, and the young man followed her on horseback. When they reached the classical bookshop at the side-gate south of the Flag Tower, she made him choose all the books he wanted, to the tune of a hundred pieces of gold. With these packed in the carriage, she drove home. She now bade him set aside all other cares, to give his whole mind to his studies. Every evening he pored over his books, with the girl at his side, and would not sleep before midnight. If she saw that he was tired, she would advise him to write a poem or ode by way of relaxation.

In two years he had thoroughly mastered his subjects, having read all the books in the kingdom. "Now I can go in for the examinations," he said.

But she answered, "No, you had better revise thoroughly, to be ready for all contingencies."

After another year, she said, "Now you may go."

He passed the examination with high distinction at

the first attempt, and his reputation spread through the Ministry of Ceremony. Even older men, when they read his compositions, felt the greatest respect for him and wanted to become his friends.

But the girl said: "Wait a little! Nowadays when a bachelor of arts has passed his examination, he thinks he deserves to become a high official and enjoy fame throughout the empire. But your shady past puts you at a disadvantage beside your fellow scholars. You must sharpen your weapons, to win a second victory. Then you can rival the best scholars."

Then the young man worked harder than ever, and his reputation grew. That year there was a special examination to select scholars of outstanding talent from all parts of the empire. The young man took the paper on criticism of the government and advice to the emperor, and came out top. He was appointed Army Inspector at Chengdu. Many high government officials were now his friends.

When he was about to take up his post, the girl said to him: "Now that you have regained your proper status, I no longer feel I have injured you. Let me go back and look after the old lady till she dies. You must marry a girl from some great family, who is fit to sacrifice to your ancestors. Don't injure yourself by an imprudent match. Take care of yourself! I must leave you."

The young man burst into tears and said: "If you leave me, I shall cut my throat."

But still she insisted that they must part.

He pleaded with her even more passionately, until she said: "Very well. I will go with you across the river as far as Jianmen. Then you must send me back."

To that he consented.

In a few weeks they reached Jianmen. Before they left a proclamation had been issued announcing that the young man's father, who had been Governor of Changzhou, had been summoned to the capital and appointed Governor of Chengdu and Inspector of Jianmen. Twelve days later, the governor of Chengdu reached Jianmen, and the young man sent in his card to the posting-station where he was staying. The Lord of Yingyang could not believe that this was his son, yet the card bore the names of the young man's father and grandfather, with their ranks and titles. He was astounded. He sent for his son and, when he arrived, fell on his neck and wept bitterly.

"Now you are my son again," he said, and asked him to tell his story. When he had heard it, the Lord of Yingyang was amazed and inquired where the girl was.

"She came this far with me," answered the young man. "But now she is going back again."

"That won't do," said his father.

The next day he took his son in his carriage to Chengdu but kept the girl at Jiamnen, finding suitable lodgings for her. The following day he ordered a go-between to arrange the wedding and prepare the six ceremonies to welcome the bride. Thus they were duly married. In the years that followed the girl proved herself a devoted wife and competent house-keeper, who was loved by all her relations.

Some years later both the young man's parents died, and he showed such filial piety in his mourning that a divine fungus appeared on the roof of his mourning-hut and the grain in that district grew three ears on each stalk. The local authorities reported this to the emperor, and informed him too that several dozen white swallows had nested in the rafters of our hero's roof. The emperor was so impressed that he immediately raised the young man's rank.

When the three years of mourning were over, he was successively promoted to various important posts. Within ten years he was governor of several provinces, while his wife was given the title Lady of Qiankuo. They had four sons, all of whom became high officials, the least successful of them becoming Governor of Taiyuan. All four sons married into great families, so that all their relations were powerful and prosperous and their good fortune was unequalled.

How amazing that a singsong girl should have shown a degree of constancy rarely surpassed by the heroines of old! It really takes one's breath away.

My great-uncle was Governor of Jinzhou, an official in the Ministry of Finance, and later Inspector of Roads and Waterways. The hero of this story was his predecessor in these three posts, so that my great-uncle knew all the details of his adventures. One day during the Zhen Yuan period (785-805), Li Gongzuo of Longxi and I happened to be talking of wives who had distinguished themselves by their integrity, and I told him the story of the Lady of Qiankuo. He listened with rapt attention, and asked me to write it down. So I took up my brush, dipped it into the ink, and jotted down this rough outline of the tale to preserve it. It was written in the eighth month of the year Yi Hai (AD 795).

Wushuang the Peerless

Xue Tiao

LIU Zhen, a courtier during the Xian Zhong period (780-783), had a nephew called Wang Xianke whom he brought up in his own family because Wang's father had died. Liu's daughter Wushuang (The Peerless) was a few years younger than Wang and the two children played together; while Liu's wife was so fond of her nephew that she gave him pet names. Several years passed, during which Liu was as kind as could be to his widowed sister and her son.

One day Wang's mother fell ill, and as she lay dying she said to Liu: "I have only this one child, and you know how I love him. I am sorry that I shan't live to see him marry. Wushuang is a beautiful, intelligent girl, and I love her dearly too. Don't marry her into any other family. I entrust my son to you. If you consent to their marriage, I shall die content."

"Set your mind at rest — you will recover," said Liu. "Don't worry about anything else." But the lad's mother died, and Wang took her coffin back to his house at Xiangyang for burial.

After the three years' mourning, he thought: "I am

Xue Tiao (830-872), a native of Hezhong (present-day Shanxi province), was a scholar of the Imperial Academy.

all alone in the world. I had better take a wife and have children. Wushuang is old enough to marry, and my uncle surely won't go back on his word even though he is now a high official." So he got his luggage ready and went to the capital.

By this time Liu was land tax commissioner and had a magnificent mansion, crowded with high-ranking visitors. When Wang called on him, Liu lodged him in the family school with his own children. But although acknowledged as his nephew, for a long time the young man heard nothing about the marriage. He had caught one glimpse of Wushuang from a window and she was as radiantly beautiful as a goddess come down to earth. He fell madly in love with her; but, afraid his uncle would not consent to their marriage, he sold all that he had to raise several million cash. With this money he tipped his uncle's and aunt's attendants and servants lavishly, and gave feasts and drinking parties until he had gained free access to the inner court of the house. He also treated the cousins among whom he lived with the greatest respect. On his aunt's birthday, he pleased her by buying novel and rare presents — trinkets of carved rhinoceros horn and jade. And about ten days later, he sent an old woman to her to ask for Wushuang's hand.

"This is what I want too," said his aunt. "We must have a talk about it."

A few days later a servant informed him, "The mistress has been talking to the master about the marriage. But, judging by the way the master behaved, there seems to be some hitch." When Wang heard this he fell into despair and could not sleep all night, for fear his uncle would refuse him. However, he went on doing his best to please him.

One day Liu went to the court but came galloping home at dawn, perspiring and out of breath, able only to gasp: "Bolt the gate! Bolt the gate!" The whole household was thrown into confusion, and no one could guess what had happened. Presently Liu told them, "The troops at Jingyuan have revolted, and Yao Ling-yan has entered the Hanyuan Hall in the imperial court with an armed force! The emperor has left the palace by the North Gate, and all his ministers have fled with him. Concern for my wife and daughter made me come back to put my affairs in order. Call Xianke at once to look after my family, and I shall marry Wushuang to him."

At this Wang was surprised and overjoyed. He thanked his uncle who, having loaded twenty baggage animals with gold, silver and silk, said to him, "Change your clothes and take these things out by Kaiyuan Gate, then hire rooms in some quiet inn. I shall bring your aunt and Wushuang after you by a roundabout route from Qixia Gate."

Wang did as he was told, waiting in an inn outside the city; but by sunset they had still not arrived, and since noonday the city gates had been closed. Tired of looking south for the arrival of his uncle's family, Wang mounted his horse and rode with a torch in his hand around the city until he came to Qixia Gate. This gate was bolted too and there were guards there holding staffs, some standing and some sitting.

"What has happened in the city?" he ventured to ask, dismounting from his horse. "Has anyone passed this way?"

"Marshal Chu Ze has made himself emperor," said one guard. "In the afternoon a richly dressed man who had four or five women with him tried to leave through this gate. Everybody in the street knew him. They said he was Liu, the land tax commissioner, so the officer in charge dared not let him pass. Later in the evening horsemen came to arrest him, and took all his family to the north part of the city."

Wang burst out sobbing, and returned to his inn. Towards midnight the city gates burst open and torches shone bright as day as shouting soldiers armed with swords and other weapons poured out to hunt down and kill any runaway courtiers. Abandoning the baggage, Wang fled in fright.

After three years spent in his country house at Xiangyang, when news came that the rebellion had been suppressed, order restored in the capital and the whole empire pacified, he returned to Chang'an to find out what had become of his uncle. He had reached the south of the Xinchang quarter and was reining in his horse, wondering where to go, when someone accosted him; and looking carefully he saw that it was his former servant Saihong. This Saihong had served Wang's father, and Liu finding him useful kept him on. Wang grasped his hand and they shed tears.

"Are my uncle and aunt well?" asked the young man.

"They are living in the Xinghua quarter," Saihong told him.

Wang was overjoyed and cried, "I shall go there then."

"I am a freeman now," said Saihong. "I am staying with a man who has a small house of his own and make a living by selling silk. It is late. You had better spend the night with me, and we can go together tomorrow." Then Saihong took him to his house where they had a good meal with plenty to drink. Later in the evening word came that, because Liu had worked for the rebels, he and his wife had been executed while Wushuang had been taken to the palace as a maid.

In his grief Wang cried aloud till all the neighbours were moved to pity.

"Wide though the world is," he told Saihong, "I have no folk of my own. Where can I go?" Then he asked, "Are there any of the old family servants left?"

"Only Wushuang's maid Caiping," replied Saihong. "She is working now in the house of General Wang, captain of the imperial guards."

"If I cannot see Wushuang again," sighed Wang, "I shall die content if only I can see her maid."

He paid a visit to the general, who had been his uncle's friend, told him the whole story from beginning to end and asked to redeem the maid with a good sum of money. The general was touched by his story, and agreed. Wang then rented a house, where he lived with Saihong and Caiping.

One day Saihong said: "Young master, you are a grown man now, you should find some official post instead of moping at home all the time." Wang let himself be persuaded, and asked the general's help. The general recommended him to City Magistrate Li, and the latter was able to have him appointed magistrate of Fuping and concurrently master of the Changle posting-station.

Several months later, a report came that a certain palace official was taking thirty handmaids to the mausoleum to set the place in good order. They would travel in ten curtained carriages and put up at the Changle posting-station.

"I hear the palace maids selected are all girls from good families," Wang told Saihong. "I wonder if Wushuang is among them. Could you find out for me?"

"There are thousands of palace maids," retorted Saihong. "Why should Wushuang be one of these?"

"Go anyway," urged Wang. "You never know."

Saihong accordingly pretended to be a station officer and went to boil tea outside the curtain of the girls' room. Wang had given him three thousand cash and told him: "Stay by the stove. Don't leave the spot. And if you see her, report to me at once." But the palace maids kept out of sight on the other side of the curtain, and could only be heard talking together at night. When it grew late and all was still, Saihong washed his bowls and stoked his fire but dared not sleep. Suddenly someone called from the other side of the curtain: "Saihong! Saihong! How did you know I was here? Is my betrothed well?" Then there was the sound of sobbing.

"Our young master is now in charge of this posting-station," said Saihong. "He thought you might be here today, so he sent me with his greetings."

"I cannot say any more now," the girl replied. "Tomorrow after we leave, you will find a letter to my betrothed under the purple quilt in the northeast pavilion." After saying this she moved away. Presently he heard a great commotion inside and cries of "She has fainted!" The officer in charge shouted for a cordial. It was Wushuang who had fainted.

Saihong hurried to report this to Wang, who in desperation demanded, "How can I see her?"

"Wei Bridge is under repair," suggested Saihong.

"You might pretend to be the officer in charge and stand near where the carriages pass. When Wushuang recognizes you, she will draw the curtain and you will see her."

Wang did as Saihong proposed. When the third carriage passed, the curtain was drawn and the sight of Wushuang filled him with grief and longing. Meantime Saihong had found the letter under the quilt in the pavilion. There were five sheets of paper with a print-ed design covered with the girl's writing and telling all that had befallen her and her utter misery. Wang shed bitter tears as he read it, certain in his heart that they would never meet again. But in a postscript to the letter she wrote, "I have heard that a bailiff named Gu in Fuping is a man you can turn to in trouble. Could you ask him to help?"

Wang requested his superior officer to relieve him of his duty at the posting-station, and went back to serve as magistrate of Fuping. He called on Bailiff Gu in his country house then for a whole year paid him frequent visits and tried in every way to please him, making him innumerable presents of embroidered silk and precious jewels. But not a word did he breathe all that time of his request. And when his term of office expired, he stayed on in the county.

One day Gu came to see him and said, "I'm a rough soldier, getting on in years. There's not much I can do for anyone. But you have treated me well, and I feel you must want something of me. I have a sense of chivalry, and I appreciate your friendship so much I mean to repay you even if it costs me my life."

Wang shed tears and bowed, then told him the whole story. When he had heard it, Gu looked up at the sky and clapped his head with his hand several times. "This is very difficult!" he exclaimed. "I shall try to help, but don't expect quick results."

Wang bowed again and responded, "If I can only see her again alive, I don't mind how long I have to wait."

Half a year passed without any news. Then one day there came a knock at Wang's door and a letter was delivered from Gu, which said, "My envoy to Mao Mountain has returned. Come over." Wang galloped there at once, but Gu said nothing. When asked about his envoy, he replied, "I have killed him. Drink some tea." Later that night he asked, "Do you have a maid in your house who knows Wushuang?" Wang told him that Caiping did and at once had her brought there. After looking her over carefully, Gu smiled approvingly and said, "I shall borrow her for a few days. You may go back now."

A few days later it was rumoured that some high official had passed through the county, and one of the palace maids had been put to death. Filled with misgivings, Wang asked Saihong to make inquiries, and found that the girl executed was Wushuang. He wept and sobbed. "I had hoped that Gu could help," he sighed, "but now she is dead! What shall I do?" He shed tears and groaned, unable to restrain himself.

That same night, after midnight, Wang heard violent knocking at the door and when he opened it found Gu there with a stretcher.

"This is Wushuang," Gu told him. "To all appearances she is dead, but her heart is still warm. She will revive tomorrow, and you can give her some medicine. But you keep this quiet!" Wang carried the girl inside and kept watch. At dawn her limbs grew warm and she opened her eyes, but the sight of Wang made her cry out and faint away. He tended her and gave her cordials till night, when she recovered.

Gu told Wang, "Today I am repaying your kindness in full. I heard that a priest in Mao Mountain had a strange drug. Anyone who takes it appears to die suddenly but actually revives within three days. So I sent someone to ask for it, and managed to get one pill. Yesterday I asked Caiping to disguise herself as an imperial envoy and give Wushuang this pill, ordering her to commit suicide because she was connected with the rebel party. At the mausoleum I pretended to be a relative, and redeemed her body with a hundred bolts of silk. I had to give big bribes to all the people on the way, to avoid being discovered. You must not stay here any longer. Outside the door you will find ten porters, five horses and two hundred bolts of silk. Take Wushuang away with you before dawn, changing your names and covering up your tracks to avoid trouble."

Before daybreak, Wang and Wushuang left. They travelled through the gorges until they reached Jiangling, where they stayed for some time. When they heard nothing from the capital to alarm them, Wang took his wife back to his country house at Xiangyang, where they remained all their life and where they had many children.

There are many vicissitudes, strange encounters and separations in human life, but I have heard of nothing comparable to this story, which I often say is unique in history. Wushuang lost her freedom during troubled times, but Wang remained loyal to his love and finally won her, thanks to the strange measures taken by Gu. After overcoming so many difficulties, the young couple were eventually able to escape and return to their home, where they lived happily as husband and wife for fifty years. A remarkable story!

The Man with the Curly Beard

Du Guangting

WHEN Emperor Yang of the Sui dynasty (605-618) visited Yangzhou, Councillor Yang Su was ordered to guard the West Capital. Now Yang Su, that proud noble, plumed himself on the fact that in those unsettled times no one in the empire had greater power or prestige than he. Giving free rein to his love of luxury and pride, he ceased to behave like a subject. He received both officials and guests seated on a couch, and went about supported by beautiful maids, in his behaviour usurping the emperor's prerogatives. He became worse, too, in his old age when, forgetting his duty to his sovereign, he made no attempt to save the realm from utter ruin.

One day Li Jing, later to become the Duke of Wei but then a private citizen, asked for an interview in order to offer advice on government policy. Yang Su, as usual, received him sitting. Li approached and said with a bow, "The empire is in a turmoil and the bold are contending for power. As chief councillor to the imperial

Du Guangting (850-933) was a native of Chuzhou (present-day Zhejiang province) who studied Taoism at Wutai Mountain in Shanxi and later lived as a hermit in Qingcheng Mountain, Sichuan. Du is reputed to have written many books, but only a few of his stories have come down to us.

house, Your Highness should be thinking of how to rally good men, and should not receive visitors sitting."

Yang Su was impressed and stood up to apologize. After talking with Li he was very pleased with him and accepted his memorandum.

Now while Li had been discoursing brilliantly, one of Yang's maids — a very beautiful girl who was standing in front of them holding a red whisk — had watched him intently. When he was leaving, she said to the officer at the door, "Ask him his name and where he lives." Li told the officer. The girl nodded and withdrew, and Li went back to his hostel.

That night, just before dawn, there was a soft knocking at Li's door, and when he got up he found a stranger there in a cap and a purple gown, who was carrying a stick and a bag. Asked who he was, the stranger said, "I am the maid with the red whisk in Councillor Yang's house." Then Li quickly let her in. When she took off her outer gown and cap, he saw she was a beautiful girl of about nineteen with a fair complexion, dressed in bright clothes. She bowed to him, and he returned the bow.

"I have served Yang Su for a long time," said the girl, "and seen many visitors. But there has never been any one like you. The vine cannot grow by itself, but needs a tree to cling to. So I have come to you."

"But Councillor Yang has great power in the capital; how can it be done?" said Li.

"Never mind him — he's an old imbecile," she replied. "Many maids have left, knowing that he will fall; and he makes very little effort to get them back. I have thought it over carefully. Don't you worry." Asked her name, she told Li it was Zhang, and that she was the eldest in her family. He found her an angel in complexion, manner, speech and character. Both happy and alarmed at this unexpected conquest, he had not a moment's peace of mind. Inquisitive people kept peeping through his door, and for a few days a half-hearted search was made for her. Then Li and the girl dressed in fine clothes and fled on horseback from the capital to Taiyuan.

On the way they stopped at a hostel in Lingshi. The bed was made, meat was boiling in the pot, Zhang was combing her long hair in front of the bed and Li was currying the horses at the door, when suddenly a man of medium height with a curly red beard rode up on a sorry-looking donkey. He threw down his leather bag before the fire, took a pillow and lay down on the bed to watch the girl comb her hair. Furious but uncertain what course to take, Li went on grooming the horses. The girl looked intently at the stranger's face, holding her hair in one hand while with the other she signed to Li behind her back to prevent his flaring up. Then, quickly pinning up her hair, she curtseyed to the stranger and asked his name. Still lying on the bed, he answered that it was Zhang.

"My name is Zhang too," she said. "We may be cousins." With a bow she asked his position in the family, and he told her he was the third child. When she informed him that she was the eldest in her family, the stranger laughed and replied, "Then you are the eldest of my younger cousins."

"Come and meet my cousin," she called to Li, who bowed to him and sat down with them by the fire.

"What are you boiling?" asked the stranger.

"Mutton. It should be cooked by now."

"I am famished," said the man with the curly beard. While Li went out to buy bread, he took a dagger from his waist and cut up the mutton. They ate together, and after they had finished the stranger sliced up what was left and gave it to the donkey. He was very quick in all his movements.

"You seem a poor fellow," the stranger remarked to Li. "How did you get hold of such a marvellous girl?"

"I may be poor but I am no fool," said Li. "I wouldn't tell anyone else, but I won't hide anything from you." And he described how it had come about.

"Where are you going now?" asked the other.

"To Taiyuan," said Li.

"By the way, I have come uninvited: have you any wine?"

Li told him that west of the hostel was a wineshop, and fetched him a pint of wine. As they ate together, he said to Li: "Judging by your looks and behaviour, you are a stout fellow. Do you know anybody remarkable in Taiyuan?"

"I used to know a man whom I thought truly great," replied Li. "My other friends are only fit to be generals and captains."

"What is his name?"

"His name is Li too."

"How old is he?"

"Only twenty."

"What is he now?"

"He is the son of a provincial general."

"He sounds like the man I am looking for," said the stranger. "But I will have to see him to make sure. Can you arrange a meeting?"

"I have a friend named Liu Wenjing who knows

him well," said Li. "We can arrange an interview through Liu. But why do you want to see him?"

"An astrologer told me there had been a strange portent at Taiyuan, and I should look into it. You are leaving tomorrow — when will you arrive?"

Li calculated how long it would take, and the stranger said, "Meet me at daybreak the day after you arrive at Fenyang Bridge." Then he got on his donkey and made off so swiftly that he was at once lost to sight.

Li and the girl were both amazed and delighted. "Such a brave fellow will not deceive us," they said. "We need not worry." After some time they whipped up their horses and left.

On the appointed day they entered the city of Taiyuan, and were very pleased to meet the stranger again. They went to find Liu, and told him, "A good fortune-teller wants to meet Li Shimin.* Will you send for him?" Liu thought highly of Li, so he immediately sent a messenger to him asking him to come. Presently Li Shimin arrived, wearing neither coat nor shoes, but with a fur coat thrown over him. He was overflowing with good spirits, and his appearance was very striking.

The curly-bearded man, sitting silently at the end of the table, was struck from the moment of his entry. After drinking a few cups with him he called Li aside and said, "This is undoubtedly the future emperor." When Li told Liu this, the latter was overjoyed and highly pleased with himself too.

After Li Shimin had left, the man with the curly beard declared, "I am eighty per cent certain, but my friend the Taoist priest must see him too. You two go

* The founder of the Tang empire, who reigned 627-649.

back to the capital, but meet me one afternoon at the wineshop east of Mahang. If you see this donkey and another lean one, that means my priestly friend and I are there, and you can go straight up." Then he left, and again they did as they were told.

On the appointed day they went to the wineshop and saw the two donkeys. Lifting up the skirts of their robes they went upstairs, and found the curly-bearded man and a priest drinking there. They were pleased to see Li, asked him to sit down and drank about a dozen cups together.

"Downstairs in the cupboard," said the man with the curly beard, "you will find a hundred thousand cash. Get a quiet place to lodge your wife, and meet me again another day at Fenyang Bridge."

When Li went to the bridge, he found the priest and the curly-bearded man already there, and they went together to see Liu. They discovered him playing chess, and after greeting him they started chatting. Liu sent a note to invite Li Shimin to watch the game. The priest played with Liu, while the curly-bearded man and Li watched.

When Li Shimin arrived, his appearance struck awe into them all. He bowed and sat down, looking so serene and talking so well that the atmosphere seemed to freshen and splendour to be shed all around. At the sight of him the priest had turned pale, and as he made his next move he said, "It's all up with me. I have lost the game, and there's no help for it. What more is there to say?" He stopped playing and took his leave. Once outside he said to the curly-bearded man, "There is no place for you in this country. You had better try your luck elsewhere. Don't give up or lose hope." They decided to leave for the capital.

To Li the curly-bearded man said, "The day after you arrive, come with your wife to my humble lodgings. I know you have no property. I want to introduce my wife to you and talk things over. Be sure not to fail me." Then he sighed and left.

Li rode back to his lodgings. Later he went with his wife to the capital to call on the curly-bearded man. The latter's house had a small, plain wooden door. When they knocked, a man opened the door, bowed to them and said, "The master has been looking forward to your arrival for a long time." They were led through inner doors, each more magnificent than the last. Forty girl attendants stood in the court, and twenty slaves led the way to the east hall where they found a great display of rare and precious objects. There were so many fine caskets, cupboards, head-dresses, mirrors and trinkets that they felt they had left the world of men. After they had washed they changed into rich and strange garments, and then their host was announced. He came in wearing a gauze cap, with a fur coat thrown over him, his whole appearance magnificent and kingly. When they had greeted each other cordially, he called his wife to come out, and they discovered that she was a beauty too. They were invited into the central hall, where there was a fine feast spread — richer than the banquets given by princes — and while they feasted twenty women musicians played music which sounded as if made in paradise. When they had eaten their fill, wine was served. Then servants carried out from the east hall twenty couches covered with embroidered silk. They removed the covers, and Li saw that the couches were laden with account books and keys.

"This is all the treasure I possess," said the man with the curly beard. "I turn it all over to you. I meant to make my mark in the world, and fight with brave men for ten years or more to carve out a kingdom. But now that the true sovereign has been found, why should I stay here? Your friend Li Shimin of Taiyuan will be a truly great ruler, who will restore peace to the empire after three or four years. With your outstanding gifts, if you do your best under his serene guidance, you will certainly reach the top rank of councillors. And your wife with her great beauty and discernment will win fame and honour through her illustrious husband. Only a woman like her could recognize your talent, and only a man like you could bring her glory. An able minister is bound to find a wise monarch. It is no accident that when the tiger roars the wind blows, and when the dragon bellows the clouds gather. You can use my gifts to help the true monarch and achieve great deeds. Go to it! Ten years from now, several hundred miles southeast of China, strange happenings will take place — that will be when I realize my ambition. When that time comes, will you both drink towards the southeast to congratulate me?" He bid his servants pay their respects to Li and his wife, saying, "From now on they are your master and mistress." Then the curly-bearded man and his wife put on military uniform and rode off, attended by one slave only. Soon they were out of sight.

Taking over the curly-bearded man's house, Li became wealthy and used his fortune to help Li Shimin to conquer the whole empire.

During the Zhen Guan period (627-649), while Li was left minister and acting prime minister, the southern tribesmen reported that a thousand big ships and one hundred thousand armed troops had entered the kingdom of Fuyu, killed the king and occupied the land. By now all was peaceful there again. Li realized that the curly-bearded man had succeeded. On his return from court he told his wife, and they put on ceremonial dress and drank to the southeast to congratulate their old friend.

From this we see that imperial power is not won by any great man who aspires to it, let alone any man who is not great. Any subject who vainly attempts to rebel is like a praying mantis dashing itself against the wheel of a chariot, for Heaven has willed that our empire should prosper for a myriad generations.

It has been suggested that much of Li's military strategy was taught him by the man with the curly beard.

The Kunlun Slave

Pei Xing

DURING the Da Li period (766-779) there was a young man called Cui, a palace guard of the Thousand Bulls Order, whose father was a high official and a close friend of a minister. One day his father told him to call on the minister to ask after his health. Now Cui was a handsome young man, rather bashful and quiet but with a very good manner. The minister ordered his maidservants to raise the curtains and ask him in. And as Cui bowed and delivered his father's message, the minister took a fancy to him; accordingly he made him sit down and talk.

There were three ravishingly beautiful maids there, who peeled red peaches into golden bowls, then poured sweetened cream over the peaches and presented them. The minister ordered one maid who was dressed in red to take a bowl to Cui; but the young man was too shy in the presence of girls to eat. Then the minister ordered the girl in red to feed him with a spoon, and Cui was forced to eat a peach while the girl smiled teasingly.

Pei Xing lived during the second half of the ninth century. He wrote or compiled three books of stories dealing mainly with fairies and spirits.

During the Tang dynasty, slaves brought to China from the South Seas were commonly known as Kunlun slaves.

When the youth rose to go, the minister said, "Come again when you have time. Don't stand on ceremony." He told the girl in red to see him out. Cui looked back at her as he left the courtyard, and she raised three fingers, turned up the palm of one hand three times, then pointed to the little mirror she wore on her breast and said, "Remember!"

When Cui had given his father an account of his visit, he went back to his study lost in thought. He became silent and low-spirited, and rapt in sad thoughts would eat nothing. All he did was to chant a poem:

> Led by chance to a fairy mountain,
> I gazed into star-bright eyes.
> Through a red door the moon is shining,
> There forlorn a white beauty lies.

None of his servants knew what was on his mind. But there was a Kunlun slave in his family called Melek who watched him for a time, then asked:

"What is troubling you that you look so sad all the time? Why not tell your old slave?"

"What do fellows like you understand?" retorted Cui. "Why pry into my private affairs?"

"Just tell me," urged Melek, "and I promise to get you what you want, be it far or near."

Impressed by his confident tone, Cui told him the whole story. "That's simple," said Melek. "Why didn't you tell me earlier, instead of moping like that?"

When Cui told him what signs the girl had made, Melek said, "That's easy to understand. When she raised three fingers, she meant that there are ten rooms in the minister's house where the maids live, and she lives in the third room. When she turned up one palm three times, she was showing fifteen fingers, for the fifteenth of the month. And the little mirror on her breast stood for the full moon on the night of the fifteenth. That is when she wants you to go to her."

Cui was overjoyed. "Is there any way for me to satisfy my longing?" he asked.

Melek smiled and said, "Tomorrow night is the fifteenth. Give me two lengths of dark blue silk to make two tightly fitting suits. The minister keeps a fierce dog to guard the girls' quarters and kill any stranger who attempts to break in. It is one of the famous Haizhou breed, swift as lightning and fierce as a tiger. I am the only man in the world who can kill this hound. Tonight I shall beat it to death for you."

Cui gave him meat and wine and next evening he left, carrying an iron hammer with chains attached to it. After the time it takes for a meal he came back, saying, "The dog is dead. Now there is nothing to stop us."

Just before midnight, the slave helped Cui to put on his dark blue suit, and with the young man on his back vaulted over about a dozen walls until they came to the girls' quarters. They stopped at the third room. The carved door was not locked, and the bronze lamp inside shed a faint light. They heard the girl sigh as she sat there expectantly. She was putting on emerald ear-rings and her face was newly rouged, but there was sadness in her face as she chanted:

> Oh, the oriole cries as she longs for her love,
> Who beneath the bright buds stole her jewel
>   away;

*Now the blue sky is cold and no message has
    come,*
So she plays her jade flute every sorrowful day.

The guards were asleep and all was quiet. Cui lifted
the curtain and entered. For a moment the girl was
speechless; then she jumped off the couch and grasping
Cui's hand said, "I knew a clever man like you would
understand the signs I made with my fingers. But by
what magic art did you come here?"

Cui told her all the planning had been done by
Melek, and that the Kunlun slave had carried him
there.

"Where is Melek?" asked the girl.

"Outside the curtain," he answered.

Then she asked Melek in, and offered him wine in
a golden bowl.

"I come from the northern borderland and my family
used to be rich," the girl told Cui. "But my present
master was commander of the army there and forced
me to be his concubine. I am ashamed that I could
not kill myself and had to live on in disgrace. Though
I powder and rouge my face, my heart is always sad.
We have fine food in jade utensils and incense in golden
censers; we wear the softest silk and sleep under embroidered coverlets, and we have mother-of-pearl screens
and jewels. Yet these things cannot make me happy,
when all the time I feel I am a prisoner. Since your
servant has this strange skill, why not rescue me from
my jail? If I were free again, I could die content.
But I would like to be your slave, and have the honour
of serving you. What do you say, sir?"

Cui changed colour and said nothing, but Melek answered, "If your mind is made up, it is quite simple."

The girl was overjoyed.

Melek asked first to be allowed to take out her baggage. After he had made three trips, he said, "I fear it will soon be dawn." Then with Cui and the girl on his back he vaulted over about a dozen high walls, just as when they had come in. And all the time the minister's guards heard nothing. Finally they returned to Cui's quarters, and hid the girl there.

The next morning, when the minister's household discovered that the girl was gone and the dog was dead, the minister was appalled. "My house is always well guarded and locked," he said, "yet now someone seems to have flown in and out leaving no trace. This must be the work of no common adventurer. Don't·let word of this get out, for fear harm should come of it."

The girl remained hidden in Cui's house for two years. Then, one spring day when she rode in a small carriage to Qujiang to see the flowers, she was recognized by one of the minister's household. When the minister learned of her whereabouts, he was amazed and summoned Cui to question him. In fear and trembling, the young man dared not conceal the truth, but told the minister the whole story and how he had been carried there by his slave.

"It was very wrong of the girl," said the minister. "But since she has served you so long, it is too late to demand justice. However I feel in duty bound to get rid of your Kunlun slave: that man is a public menace."

Then he ordered fifty guards, armed to the teeth, to surround Cui's house and capture the Kunlun slave. But Melek, a dagger in his hand, vaulted over the wall as swiftly as if he had wings, like some huge bird of prey. Though arrows rained down, they all fell short, and in a flash he made good his escape.

Cui's family was thrown into a panic. The minister too regretted what he had done, and was afraid. Every night for a whole year he had himself guarded by servants armed with swords and halberds.

Over ten years later, one of Cui's household saw Melek selling medicine in the market at Luoyang. He looked as vigorous as ever.

The General's Daughter

Pei Xing

NIE Yinniang was the daughter of Nie Feng, a general of Weibo during the Zhen Yuan period (785-805). When she was ten, a nun came to her father's house to beg for alms and took a fancy to the girl — she asked to have her as a pupil.

General Nie flew into a passion and stormed at her.

But the nun said: "Even if you lock her up in an iron chest, I shall steal her."

That night, sure enough, Yinniang disappeared. In great dismay, her father ordered a search to be made, but no trace could be found of her. Each time the parents thought of their daughter, they looked at each other and shed tears.

Five years later, the nun brought Yinniang back and told the general: "Now I have taught her, you may have her again." This said, she vanished.

The whole family wept for joy and asked the girl what she had learned.

"At first I simply read sutras and magic chants," she said. "That was all."

General Nie did not believe this and begged for the truth.

"If I tell the truth, you may not credit it," she warned him.

"Never mind. Let's hear it," he replied.

She said: "When the nun first carried me off, we travelled I don't know how many *li*. By morning we had come to a great cave several dozen paces across. No one lived in it, but there were many monkeys about and the place was overgrown with pines and creepers. There were two girls too who were also about ten and both intelligent and pretty. They ate nothing but could skim up sheer cliffs as nimbly as any monkey climbing a tree, not slipping once. The nun gave me a pill and a sword about two feet long, with a blade so sharp that a hair blown against it was cut in two. She ordered me to follow the two girls, and little by little I felt myself grow as light as air. After a year I could hunt monkeys and not miss one in a hundred. Then I hunted tigers and leopards, coming back with their heads. Three years later I could fly and strike at eagles, without missing a single one. By degrees the blade of the sword was reduced to five inches, and the birds I went for did not even know it was coming. In the fourth year, the nun left the two girls in charge of the cave while she took me to a city — just where, I don't know. She would point a man out and list his crimes, then say:

'Now go and cut off his head for me without anyone knowing. Just be bold, and it will be as easy as catching birds.'

"She gave me a horn-handled dagger three inches long so that I could kill men in broad daylight in the streets unseen. I used to put the heads in a bag, and back in her lodging they would be changed into water by means of some drug. In the fifth year the nun told me that a certain powerful official was guilty of murdering several innocent people. She sent me at night to his house to cut off his head. I took the dagger and went there, creeping through a crack of the door without difficulty and hiding myself on the beam. But when I took his head back that night, the nun was very angry.

" 'Why did you take so long?' she demanded.

"I told her I hadn't the heart to kill him because I saw him playing with a dear little boy.

"The nun ordered me: 'Next time such a thing happens, first kill the one he loves and then behead him.' After I had apologized she said: 'I shall slit the back of your head to hide your dagger there, but it won't hurt. When you need it, you can take it out.' Then she said: 'Now that you have learned your art, you can go home.' As I was leaving, she told me: 'Twenty years from now we shall meet again.' "

This story struck dread into the general's heart.

After that, Yinniang disappeared every night and did not return till the morning. Her father, who dared not ask where she had been, could not love her as before.

One day a young mirror-polisher came to their gate.

"This man will do for my husband," Yinniang said.

Her father when she told him did not like to refuse, and so the two were married. Since her husband was fit for nothing but polishing mirrors, the general kept them well supplied with food and clothing, lodged in a separate house.

A few years later Yinniang's father died, and the Military Governor of Weibo, who had heard something of her strange arts, gave her a stipend and appointed her an assistant officer. So several years passed.

In the Yuan He period (806-821), the Military Governor of Weibo fell out with Liu Changyi, Military Governor of Chenxu, and sent Yinniang off to Chenxu to fetch his head. But Governor Liu, who was a diviner and knew that she was coming, ordered his officer to wait the next day north of the city for a man and woman who would ride up to the city gate on white and black donkeys. A magpie would start chattering in front of them and the man would shoot at the bird with his catapult but miss it, after which his wife would snatch the catapult from him and kill the magpie with one shot. Then the officer should bow to them and inform them that he had been sent by the governor, who wished to see them.

The officer, doing as he was told, met Yinniang and her husband.

"Governor Liu must have magic powers," they said. "How otherwise could he have known that we were coming? We would like to meet him."

Governor Liu welcomed them, and Yinniang and her husband bowed to him.

"We deserve a thousand deaths for meaning to harm you," they said.

"Not at all," replied Liu. "It is natural for men to serve their own master. But this district is just as good as your own: I hope you will stay here without distrust."

Yinniang thanked him, saying: "Since you have no helpers we would like to come here, for we are overwhelmed by your divine wisdom." She knew that the Governor of Weibo was not his equal. When Liu asked what they would need, she said: "Two hundred cash a day will be sufficient." He granted this request.

The two donkeys disappeared, and though Liu had a search made they could not be found. Later he discovered a cloth bag with two paper donkeys in it, one white and one black.

When more than a month had passed, Yinniang reported to Liu: "Since the Governor of Weibo does not know that we are staying here, he may send someone else. Tonight I shall put some of my hair tied up in a red handkerchief by his pillow to show that I am not going back." To this Liu agreed.

At the fourth watch she returned to report: "I have let him know. Still, two nights from now he will send Spirit Boy to kill me and cut off your head. But I shall do my best to kill him. There is no need to worry."

Since Liu was brave and broad-minded he showed no fear.

That night candles were lit and after midnight Liu saw two pennants, one red and one white, fluttering in the air as they fought around his bed. After some time a decapitated man fell from the air and Yinniang, appearing at the same instant, announced: "Spirit Boy is killed!"

She dragged the corpse out of the hall and used her drug to change it into water, leaving not a hair behind.

Then she told Liu: "Two nights from now they will send magic-fingered Empty Boy along. He has miraculous powers, this Empty Boy. Neither man nor spirit can trace his whereabouts, for he vanishes into empty air without form or shadow. My art is no match for his: we shall have to count more on your luck. Protect your neck with jade from Khotan and wrap yourself well in your bedding. I shall change into an insect and lie in wait for him concealed in your body. That is our only chance."

Liu did as she said.

That night at midnight he had not yet dozed off when something clattered sharply against his neck. The next moment Yinniang leaped out of his mouth and congratulated him, saying: "Your worries are over! This fellow is like a fine falcon, if he fails to catch his prey he goes far away, too ashamed to try again. Within a couple of hours he will be a thousand *li* from here."

When Liu examined the jade, he found a deep gash in it. After that he treated Yinniang even more handsomely.

In the eighth year of the Yuan He period (AD 814), Liu left his post to go to court, but Yinniang did not choose to accompany him.

"I shall roam the hills and river banks to find exceptional men," she said. "But may I ask for a subsidy for my husband?"

After Liu had granted this she disappeared without a trace.

When Liu died at his post, Yinniang rode to the capital on her donkey to mourn before his coffin.

During the Kai Cheng period (836-841), Liu's son Zong was appointed prefect of Lingzhou, and on his way through the mountains to Chengdu he met Yinniang, looking exactly as before, still riding her white donkey. Though pleased to see him, she warned him: "A great calamity is in store for you if you stay here." She produced a pill and told him to eat it, saying: "Your only hope lies in giving up your office next year and posting back to Luoyang. This drug cannot protect you for more than one year."

Not altogether convinced, Zong offered her silk, but Yinniang declined the gift. After drinking heavily with him, she went away. The next year Zong did not resign, but met his death in Lingzhou. As for Yinniang, she was never seen again.

The Jade Mortar and Pestle

Pei Xing

DURING the Chang Qing period (821-824), a scholar named Pei Hang, who had failed in the examination, roamed the country till he came to Ezhu where he called on his old friend Minister Cui.   When the minister gave him two hundred thousand cash, he determined to go back to the capital and took a passage on a large junk which was sailing up the River Han. Another passenger, Madame Fan, was a most beautiful lady.   They exchanged remarks across a curtain, chatting quite freely; but though so close, Pei Hang could not meet her face to face. So he bribed her maid Misty Wreath to deliver this poem to her:

> *Were we as far apart as Hu and Yue,* I would*
> *   still long to meet you;*
> *But all that divides me from you, goddess, is a*
> *   silk screen;*
> *If you are bound for the Jade City of the im-*
> *   mortals,*
> *Let me follow your phoenix train up the azure*
> *   sky!*

---

* Referring to the Huns in the north and the State of Yue in the south.

For long he received no answer to this poem. He cross-questioned Misty Wreath several times, till she said: "What can I do if my lady chooses to ignore it?"

At his wit's end, Pei purchased good wine and choice fruit next time they stopped, and presented these to Madame Fan, who then told Misty Wreath to admit him. When the curtain was raised, he saw a beauty cold and bright as jade, lovely as a flower, with hair like clouds and eyebrows like the crescent moon. She behaved like a being from above who had condescended to visit a mere mortal. Pei Hang bowed and was lost in wonder at her beauty.

The lady said, "I have a husband south of the River Han who means to resign from office to live as a hermit in the hills. He has summoned me to bid farewell. Overwhelmed with grief and with anxiety lest I fail to reach him in time, what eyes can I have for others? I have enjoyed your company on the boat, sir, but I am in no mood for trifling."

"I would not dream of such a thing!" he replied.

After drinking with him, she withdrew. She was as cold as ice, as forbidding as frost. Later she sent Misty Wreath to him with this poem:

> Drinking your wine I was deeply moved;
> Once the elixir is well ground you shall see
>   Yunying;
> Lanqiao is the abode of immortals,
> You need not climb to the Jade City in heaven.

Pei Hang, reading this, admired her talent in versifying but could not fathom her meaning. He was not granted any more interviews, and they simply exchanged greetings through Misty Wreath. When the boat reached Xiangyang, the lady and her maid took their dressing-cases and left without bidding goodbye, and he did not know where she had gone. Though he searched everywhere for her, she had vanished utterly leaving no trace. Then he gathered together his belongings to continue his journey on horseback. At Lanqiao posting station, parched with thirst, he dismounted to ask for a drink. He found a low thatched cottage of three or four rooms, in which an old woman was spinning hempen thread. Greeting her, he begged for a drink.

"Yunying!" called the old crone. "Bring a bowl! Here's a gentleman wanting a drink."

Pei Hang was astonished, remembering the name Yunying in Madame Fan's poem. While he was trying to collect his thoughts, from behind a reed screen appeared two slender white hands holding a porcelain bowl. Pei Hang took this and drank. It was like a true essence of jade, and a wonderful fragrance came to him through the door. As he returned the bowl he threw up the door curtain and discovered a girl lovely as a flower bathed in dew or spring snow melting in the rosy sunlight. Her face was like jade but softer, her hair like thick clouds. When she turned away shyly, hiding her face, not even a crimson orchid deep in the valley could match her exquisite beauty. Pei Hang stood rooted to the ground in amazement and could not tear himself away.

He told the old woman: "My man and my horse are hungry. We would like to stay here for a while. Grant me this request and I shall pay you well."

She replied: "As you like."

When man and beast had been fed, Pei said to the old

woman, "Just now I saw a young lady of astounding loveliness, a peerless beauty. That is why I hesitated and could not go away. May I send rich gifts and marry her?"

The old woman said: "The truth is she is promised to a man but not yet married. I am old and ailing. The other day an immortal gave me an elixir, but I cannot eat it till it has been pounded for a hundred days in a jade mortar with a jade pestle. Then I can live as long as heaven. You shall marry the girl if you get me a jade mortar and pestle. I have no use for gold or silk or the like."

Pei Hang bowed in thanks, saying: "Grant me a hundred days and I promise to come back with the jade mortar and pestle. Don't let anyone else have her meantime."

The old woman agreed to this and Pei reluctantly left.

When he reached the capital he set aside other business to make the round of all the public squares, busy markets and bustling streets crying out that he wanted a jade mortar and pestle. But there was no sign of one. He ignored the friends whom he met, till he was generally thought to be out of his mind. When several months had passed he met an old jade pedlar, who told him, "Not long ago I had a letter from Old Bian who keeps a medicine shop in Guozhou. He says he has a jade pestle and mortar for sale. Since you are so eager to find one, I can give you an introduction to him."

Pei Hang thanked him heartily, for at last he would succeed in getting the mortar and pestle. Old Bian's price was two hundred strings of cash, and to raise this sum Pei had to empty his purse and sell his man and horse into the bargain. Then, taking his purchases, he returned on foot to Lanqiao.

The old woman laughed and said: "I see you are a man of your word, sir! I can't keep the girl and not reward you for your services."

The girl said with a smile, "Still, he must pound the elixir for a hundred days before we can talk of marriage."

The old woman took the elixir from her pocket and Pei Hang started pounding it, working all day and resting at night, when the old woman took the mortar to the inner room. But in the dark the sound of pounding went on; and when Pei peeped in he saw a jade hare manipulating the pestle, while a light white as snow lit up the whole room so that every little thing in it stood out clearly. This further strengthened his determination.

When the hundred days had passed the old woman took the elixir and swallowed it, saying: "I am going to a cave in the mountain to tell my relatives to prepare the bridal chamber for you." Before taking the girl with her to the hills she told Pei, "Just wait here for a little."

Soon a retinue of attendants and carriages came to fetch him. They escorted him to a great mansion which reached the clouds, with pearl-studded gates which flashed in the sunlight. Inside he found curtains, screens, jewels and precious objects of every description, far surpassing the house of a noble. Pages and maids led him behind the curtain to go through the wedding ceremony. After that he paid his respects to the old woman and expressed his regret that she was leaving them. The old woman said, "Since you are a descendant of Saint Pei,* you will leave the world too. You need not regret this."

Then he was introduced to the guests, all of whom were immortals. One goddess, who wore her hair in a knot and whose gown was the colour of the rainbow, was introduced as his wife's elder sister. When he paid his respects she asked:

"Don't you recognize me, Mr Pei?"

He said: "We are not kinsmen, and I cannot recollect meeting you."

The lady asked, "Don't you remember travelling in the same boat with me from Ezhu to Xiangyang?"

Then Pei, taken aback, apologized.

Later he learned from others: "This is your wife's elder sister, Lady Yunqiao, the wife of Lord Liu Gong.** She has already attained the rank of an angel and waits on the Jade Emperor in heaven."

The old woman sent Pei and his wife to stay in Jade Peak Cave, where he was given the Elixir of Rosy Snow and Jasper Flowers which made him ethereal: his hair turned colour, he could transform himself at will, and he became an immortal.

During the Tai He period (827-835) his friend Lu Hao met him west of Lanqiao Station. Pei told Lu how he had attained immortality and gave him ten pounds of fine jade and a pill to prolong his life. After conversing all day, he asked Lu to take his regards to his old friends.

Lu Hao bowed and said: "You have attained immortality. Can you give me some brief instructions?"

---

* An ancient Taoist saint.
** Another well-known Taoist saint.

Pei said, "Lao Zi* has taught us: 'Keep the mind empty and the belly full.' But the men of today keep their minds so full that they cannot attain immortality." When he saw that Lu was bewildered, he added: "When the mind is full of vain desires, the belly cannot retain the vital spirit — that is what I mean. All men have it in their power to attain immortality and keep the vital spirit; but the time has not yet come for you to learn this. I shall explain it to you some other day."

Lu Hao realized that he would be taught no more. After a meal Pei Hang left, and that was the last that was ever seen of him.

---

* The ancient Taoist philosopher who wrote *The Way and Its Power*.

The Prince's Tomb

Pei Xing

DURING the Zhen Yuan period (785-805) there was a certain Cui Wei, son of the Censor Cui Xiang who enjoyed some reputation as a poet and ended his career as assistant prefect of Nanhai.* This Cui Wei lived a carefree life in Nanhai, neglecting his estate but doing many gallant deeds till in a few years all his property was gone. Then for the most part he stayed in Buddhist temples. On the Zhong Yuan Festival** it was the custom in Panyu*** to display strange and precious objects in the temples, and all the showmen gathered in Kaiyuan Monastery. Cui, going there to look on, saw a stall-holder beating an old beggar woman who had tripped over his wine jug and upset it. Since the wine spilt cost no more than one string of cash and Cui pitied the old woman, he stripped off his own gown to make good the damage. But she left without a word of thanks.

The next day, however, she appeared and said: "I owe you thanks, sir, for coming to my rescue. I know how to cauterize tumours, and here is some mugwort for you from Yue Well. Any tumour you treat with this

---

* Part of the present province of Guangdong.
** The fifteenth of the seventh month.
*** Present-day Guangzhou.

will be instantly cured. You will find a beautiful wife into the bargain."

As Cui accepted with a smile, the old woman vanished.

Some days later, having strolled to Haikuang Monastery he met an old monk with a tumour on one ear. When Cui tried cauterizing this with his mugwort, it happened just as predicted. The grateful monk told Cui:

"A poor priest has no means of repaying you except by chanting prayers for your happiness, sir. But old Mr Ren, who lives at the foot of this mountain and owns millions of strings of cash, has a tumour too. If you can cure him, he will reward you well. Allow me to give you a letter of introduction." Cui fell in readily with this suggestion.

Old Mr Ren, overjoyed to see him, invited him in with all ceremony. And Cui's mugwort effected an immediate cure.

"I cannot thank you enough, sir, for ridding me of this annoyance," said Ren. "Here are a hundred thousand cash for you. Pray make this your home. Don't be in any hurry to leave." So Cui stayed in their house.

Now Cui had a gift for music. When he heard a lyre played outside his host's hall he questioned a serving-boy about it. "That is our master's daughter," was the answer.

Then Cui asked for a lyre and made music too. And the girl's heart went out to him as, in hiding, she listened.

Old Ren worshipped a demon in his house called the One-legged God. Every three years he killed a man for it. Now the day for the sacrifice was at hand, but he had as yet found no victim. Then abruptly forgetting Cui's kindness, he called for his son and took counsel with him, saying: "Since the man I counted on hasn't come, there is no blood-offering for the demon. Even great kindness, they say, may go unrequited, and this fellow simply cured me of a minor ailment."

He ordered the sacrifice to be prepared, meaning to kill Cui at midnight. And unknown to Cui, he locked him into his room. Ren's daughter, learning of this plot, stole to Cui's window with a sword to warn him:

"My family worships a demon and tonight they mean to sacrifice you to it. Break the window with this and escape; otherwise you are a dead man. And take this sword with you, or I shall be in trouble."

Sweating with fear, Cui took the sword and his mugwort. Breaking the lattice of the window he leaped out, unlatched the gate and fled. But old Mr Ren got wind of this and gave chase with a dozen of his men carrying swords and torches. After six or seven *li* they had nearly caught up with Cui when, missing his way, he slipped and fell into a large disused well. His pursuers, losing track of him, went back.

Cui's fall had been broken by dead leaves so that no damage was done. When dawn came he saw that he was in a chasm a thousand feet and more deep, with no way out. There was space in those winding clefts for a thousand men. In the middle, in front of a stone mortar, a white snake dozens of feet long lay coiled. And into this mortar from the cliff dripped some substance like honey which the snake was drinking. Certain that this was no ordinary snake, Cui made obeisance to it.

"Dragon King!" he cried. "I have had the misfortune to fall here. Take pity on me! Spare my life!"

He swallowed the dregs of the honey, which satisfied hunger and thirst. A closer look disclosed that this snake, too, had a tumour on its mouth; and to show his gratitude he would gladly have cauterized this, but there was no way to get fire. When some time later a flame from far off drifted into the cave, Cui kindled his mugwort and with the snake's consent cauterized its tumour, which fell at once to the ground. Since this growth had long interfered with the snake's feeding, it experienced great relief and spat out a pearl about one inch across as a reward for Cui. But declining this, he said:

"Dragon King, you who control clouds and rain, whose power is infinite, who can change your form at will and go where you please — you must know some way to rescue a man in distress! If you will carry me back to the world of men, I shall be eternally grateful. If I can only go back, I want no treasure."

The snake swallowed the pearl and uncoiled itself to move on. Having bowed low, Cui mounted its back and they set off. But instead of leaving by the mouth of the chasm, they thrust several dozen *li* further into pitch darkness. The snake shed light upon both walls, however, so that from time to time they saw paintings of men of old in official dress. At last they reached a stone gate on which was a golden beast with a ring in its mouth. Inside this gate all was bright. Halting there, the snake lowered its head to let Cui alight, and believing himself near the world of men he entered. But he found a hall more than a hundred paces across with chambers hollowed out of the four walls.   In the middle were embroidered hangings of gold and purple silk adorned with pearls and emeralds to sparkle like galaxies of twinkling stars. In front of these were ranged golden incense-burners in the shape of dragons, phoenixes, tortoises, serpents and sparrows, from whose mouths issued heady, aromatic fragrance. Beside was a small pool with a golden verge, filled with quicksilver on which floated water-fowl carved out of jade, while round the pool were couches inlaid with rhinoceros horn and ivory, laden with every manner of instruments: lyres, cithers, flutes, pipes, drums, clappers and many more. Observing that these showed signs of recent handling, Cui wondered into what fairyland he had strayed. After a while he picked up a lyre to strum it. At once doors in the four walls swung open and a maid-servant appeared, who said with a smile: "So the Envoy of the Jade City has brought Mr Cui here!" With that she ran in again.

Presently four girls came out, each with her hair dressed in an antique fashion and a gown every colour of the rainbow.

"How dare you break into the emperor's inner palace?" they asked.

Cui put down the lyre and bowed. The girls returned his courtesy. "If this is the emperor's inner palace, where is the emperor?" he inquired.

"He has gone to a feast given by the Fiery Emperor Zhu Rong."*

They made Cui be seated to play the lyre, and he played *The Hunnish Pipes*.

"What tune is that?" they asked.

"*The Hunnish Pipes*."

---

* The god of the south.

"What does it mean? We've never heard it."

Cui told them: "The Han dynasty scholar Cai Rong had a daughter, Wenji, who was captured by the Huns. On her return, recalling all she had seen, she made this song on her lyre resembling the wailing of Hunnish pipes."

The girls were enchanted. "It must be a new song," they said.

They ordered wine to be poured and passed round the cups. And when Cui kowtowed and begged leave to go home, they replied, "Fate brought you here, sir. Don't be in such a hurry to leave. Stay a little while. Soon the Envoy of the City of Sheep will arrive, and you can go with him." They also told him, "The emperor has agreed to give you Lady Tian as your wife. You can see her now."

When Cui, at a loss, did not venture to reply, the girls told their maid to fetch Lady Tian. But she refused to come, sending back the answer: "I cannot meet Mr Cui till I have orders from the emperor." Though the girls insisted, she was adamant. They told Cui: "Lady Tian is matchless for beauty and virtue: You must take good care of her. This, too, is fated. She is the daughter of the Prince of Chi."

"Which Prince of Chi?" he inquired.

"That Tian Heng who lost his kingdom and fled to the isles early in the Han dynasty."

Soon rays of sunlight shone into the cave and Cui, looking up, saw an opening above and what seemed to be the sky of the world of men. The four girls said, "Here is the Envoy of the City of Sheep."

Then from the sky above a white sheep descended slowly to where they were sitting. Its rider, splendid in official robes, held a large brush and a bamboo slip inscribed with hieroglyphics, which he placed on the incense table. At the four girls' order the maid read out, "Prefect Xu Shen of Guangzhou has died. Tribune Zhao Chang of Annam will succeed to his post."

The girls poured wine for the envoy and said to him, "Mr Cui wants to return to Panyu. Will you take him with you?" The envoy agreed and turned to say to Cui: "In return some day you must give me a new coat and repair my house." Cui promised to do this.

The four girls announced: "The emperor has ordered us to present to you his great treasure, the Sunlight Pearl. When you take it back, a foreigner will give you a hundred thousand strings of cash for it." They told the maid to open a jade casket and hand the pearl to Cui. He accepted it with a bow, but said: "I have never paid my respects to His Majesty and am no relation to him. Why is such a priceless gift given to me?"

The girls answered: "Your father wrote a poem on Yue Palace which moved Prefect Xu Shen to repair it. The emperor was grateful and appended a poem, hinting that he meant to give this pearl to you. But surely you know this without our telling you?"

Cui requested: "May I hear the emperor's poem?"

The girls told the maid to write it on the envoy's pen. The poem was as follows:

> A thousand years the ruined palace mouldered
> Till thanks to the governor it was restored;
> How can I repay your welcome services?
> I shall grant you a beauty and a precious pearl.

"What was the emperor's name?" asked Cui.

"You will learn that later," said the girls. "On

the Zhong Yuan Festival prepare some good wine and a feast in a quiet room in Pujian Monastery in Guangzhou. We shall bring Lady Tian to you there."

Cui took his leave and was about to ride off on the envoy's sheep when the girls stopped him. "We know you have some of Mistress Bao's mugwort," they said. "Will you leave us a little?" Cui did as they asked, though he still had no idea who Mistress Bao could be. Then he left them and in no time was out of the cave and on firm ground. The envoy and the sheep had disappeared.

Looking at the sky, he saw it was nearly dawn. At once the Pujian Monastery bell tolled the fifth watch, and going there he was given breakfast by the monks. Then he went back to Guangzhou. Having originally had lodgings there, he went straight to his old rooms to make inquiries and found that he had been away for three years.

His landlord asked, "Where have you been all this time?" But Cui did not tell him the truth. When he opened the door and found his couch covered with dust, he felt a pang of sadness. Inquiring about the local administration, he learned that Prefect Xu had died and been succeeded by Tribune Zhao Chang. He took his pearl, well concealed, to the Persian hostel, and the moment an old merchant set eyes on it he prostrated himself with his hands spread out before him.

"You must come from the tomb of Prince Zhao Tuo of Southern Yue,* sir," he cried. "Nowhere else could you have got this treasure which was buried with him."

---

* Zhao Tuo assumed the title of prince when the Qin dynasty fell, but later acknowledged Han suzerainty.

As Cui related the story he realized that the emperor was Zhao Tuo, who had assumed this title. The price of a hundred thousand strings of cash was paid.

"How did you recognize this jewel?" Cui asked.

"This is the Sunlight Pearl which all Arabs treasure," said the merchant. "At the beginning of the Han dynasty, Zhao Tuo sent a magician over mountains and seas to steal this pearl and bring it to Panyu. That was nearly a thousand years ago. Because a soothsayer in our country foretold that next year this treasure would return to the Arabs, our king sent me with a great ship and store of money to Panyu in search of it. Today at last I have found it!" He produced an essence of jade to wash the pearl, and its brightness lit up the whole room. Then the foreigner boarded his boat and sailed back to the land of the Arabs.

Cui bought property with his money, but looked in vain for the Envoy of the City of Sheep. During a visit later to the temple of the tutelary god, he saw that the image there resembled the envoy while the deity's pen was inscribed with tiny characters — the poem written by the maid. Then he sacrificed wine and meat to the guardian deity of the city, restoring and redecorating his temple, for he realized that Guangzhou was the City of Sheep, since this temple had images of five sheep.

Next he looked for the house of old Mr Ren, and was told by the village elders that it must be the grave of Ren Xiao, Tribune of Southern Yue.* He mounted the ruined tower of the Yue Palace and found there a poem by his father:

---

* Tribune of Nanhai in the Qin dynasty, who was succeeded by Zhao Tuo.

By Yue Well stand old pine and cypress trees;
On Yue Tower autumn grass grows rank;
For years no descendants have come to this
*   ancient tomb*
Which, trampled by country folk, has become a
*   public road.*

He also found the poem appended to this by the Prince of Yue, at which he marvelled exceedingly. When questioned, the care-taker told him: "Prefect Xu Shen when he came here was so impressed by Censor Cui's poem that he restored the palace. Then this miracle happened."

When the Zhong Yuan Festival was approaching, Cui prepared a rich feast with rare dishes and good wine, and took a room in Pujian Monastery. Towards midnight the four girls escorted in Lady Tian, a ravishing beauty whose conversation was distinguished. The four girls toasted Cui and joked with each other till nearly dawn, when they took their leave. Cui, having bowed and asked them to deliver a letter of thanks to the Prince of Yue, went back into the room with Lady Tian.

"If your father was the Prince of Qi, how did you come to marry a southerner?" he asked her.

"My country fell, my home was destroyed," she said. "I was captured by the Prince of Yue, who made me his concubine. When he died, I was buried with him. How much time has passed since then I cannot tell. It seems just yesterday that Li Yiqi died in the cauldron.* Recalling the past brings tears to my eyes."

---

* Li Yiqi, an orator sent by the First Emperor of Han to persuade the Prince of Qi to come over to his side, was thrown into a cauldron by the prince.

"Who were those four girls?" asked Cui.

"Two of them were presented to the prince by Prince Yao, the other two by Prince Wu Zhu.* All four were buried with their master."

"Who was the Mistress Bao of whom they spoke?"

"The daughter of Bao Qing and the wife of Ge Hong.** She often practised cautery in the south."

Cui was astonished by this revelation. He asked next: "Why was the snake called the Envoy of the Jade City?"

She told him: "An Qisheng*** used to ride that dragon to the Jade City, hence the name."

Since Cui had drunk dregs left by the dragon in the chasm, his flesh became tender and youthful, his sinews flexible and strong. After spending more than ten years in the south, he gave away all he possessed to devote himself to a holy life. Then he and his wife went to Luofu Mountain in search of Mistress Bao. And what became of him after that no one knows.

---

* Two princes who reigned in southeastern China at the beginning of the Han dynasty.

** A famous third-century alchemist in southern China.

*** A Qin dynasty alchemist.

The Spendthrift and the Alchemist

Li Fuyan

DU Zichun, who lived at the end of the Northern Zhou dynasty (557-581) and the beginning of the Sui dynasty (581-618), was a young spendthrift who neglected his estate. Dissolute, fond of drinking and low pleasures, he soon squandered his fortune; and relatives whom he asked to take him in all turned him away because he refused to work. One winter day, ragged and hungry, he loitered till it was late at the west gate of the East Market, not knowing where to go. A picture of misery, he stood there looking up at the sky and sighing.

An old man with a stick came up and asked him, "Why are you sighing?"

Then Du poured out his indignation at his relatives' heartlessness. His face revealed his feelings.

"How much money do you need?" asked the old man.

"I could manage with thirty or forty thousand," said Du.

"That's not enough," said the old man. "Think again."

"A hundred thousand."

"That's not enough."

Li Fuyan lived in the early part of the ninth century and wrote five books of tales and anecdotes.

"A million."

"That's not enough."

"Three million."

"That's more like it," said the old man. He took some money from his sleeve and gave it to Du, saying, "This is for tonight. Tomorrow at noon I shall wait for you at the Persian Hostel in the West Market. Be sure to come on time."

Du went there punctually the next day, and sure enough the old man gave him three million cash, but then left without disclosing his name.

Now that he was rich, Du became a spendthrift once more, confident that this vagabond life was over. He bought fine horses and rich clothes, and gathered boon companions to enjoy music and dancing in the courtesans' quarter. Not once did it occur to him to invest his money. In a couple of years he had nothing left and had to sell his rich clothes, carriages and horses to buy cheaper ones. Eventually he sold his last horse and bought a donkey, then sold his donkey to go on foot, until soon he was as destitute as ever.

Once again he did not know what to do, and could only lament his fate at the market gate. At once the old man appeared, grasped his hand and said, "What! Are you reduced to this again? Tell me how much you need, and I will help you."

Du was ashamed to answer, and although the old man pressed him he kept declining. At last the old man said, "Come tomorrow at noon to where we met before."

Du did so, in spite of his shame, and received ten million cash. Before accepting, he was determined to turn over a new leaf and go into business so that he could outdo the richest men of old. But with money in his hands, he forgot his good resolutions and became as fond of pleasures as before. So in three or four years he was poorer than ever and once again met the old man in the same place. Overcome with shame, Du hid his face and turned to go, but the old man took hold of his coat and stopped him, saying, "How badly you manage!" With that he gave him another thirty million, and said, "If this does not cure you, you must be beyond saving."

Du thought, "I have led a dissolute life and run through all my property, and none of my relatives has ever helped me. Now here is this old man who has given me money three times — how can I repay him?" So he said to the old man, "With this sum I can settle my worldly affairs, make provision for my poor relatives and fulfil all my obligations. I am deeply grateful to you. After my affairs are settled, I shall do whatever you tell me."

"That is what I wish," was the old man's reply. "After you have settled your affairs, meet me on the fifteenth of the seventh month next year under the twin juniper trees in front of the Taoist temple."

As most of Du's poor relatives lived in the southern Huai River valley, he bought more than one thousand five hundred acres of land near Yangzhou, erected mansions in the suburbs of the city and built more than a hundred country villas by the chief highways. Having settled his poor relations there, he arranged marriages for his nephews and nieces and moved back to the ancestral burial place all members of the clan who had been buried outside. He repaid all who had helped him, too, and settled scores with old enemies. This done, he went to the temple on the date appointed.

He found the old man singing in the shade of the twin juniper trees, and together they set out for Yuntai Peak on Hua Mountain. After they had walked about fifteen miles they came to an imposing mansion which was obviously not the home of any common man. Bright clouds hovered over it and phoenixes and storks were flying there. In the central hall was a cauldron over nine feet high in which drugs were being brewed, and the purple flame cast a bright light on the windows. Around the cauldron stood magic figures of the Jade Virgins, the Green Dragons and the White Tigers.

It was now nearly sunset, and the old man took off his ordinary dress and revealed himself as a priest in a yellow cap and red cape. He gave Du three white marble pills and a goblet of wine, then made him sit on a tiger skin by the west wall, facing east. "Be sure not to say a word!" he warned him. "Not even if you see deities, devils, vampires, wild beasts, the horrors of hell, or your relatives bound and in agony — it will all be an illusion. But you must neither speak nor stir. Have no fear, for no harm will come to you. At all costs, remember what I have said." With that he disappeared. When Du looked round the hall, he saw nothing but a huge jar filled with water.

The priest had no sooner gone than thousands of chariots and horsemen swept over the hills and valleys with flags flying and weapons gleaming. Their battle cries shook heaven and earth. Their commander was over ten feet in height and both he and his charger were in gilded armour which dazzled the eye. This giant led several hundred warriors straight to the hall, where they unsheathed their swords and stretched taut their bows. "Who are you?" the commander roared at Du. "How dare you confront me?" All the warriors rushed forward with drawn swords to demand Du's name and reason for being there. But he said not a word. This so enraged them that furious yells of "Shoot him! Kill him!" resounded like thunder. Still he said not a word, and finally the commander withdrew, fuming with rage.

Then fierce tigers, deadly dragons, griffins, lions and tens of thousands of cobras rushed forward roaring and hissing, threatening to swallow Du up or throw themselves on him. But not a muscle of his face moved, and soon these monsters vanished too.

Then torrential rain fell and the day grew dark. Lightning flashed around him and thunderbolts crashed beside him, until he could not open his eyes. The courtyard was presently more than ten feet deep in water which poured swift as lightning, loud as thunder, and irresistible as a deluge into the hall. In a flash the water had reached him. But Du sat there ignoring it till the flood vanished too.

Then the commander returned, leading ox-headed jailers and other foul fiends from hell. They set a boiling cauldron before Du and hemmed him in with long spears, swords and prongs. "If he will tell his name, let him go," ordered the commander. "Otherwise, run him through and throw him into the cauldron."

Still he said nothing.

Then they brought in his wife and threw her down at the foot of the steps leading to the hall. Pointing to her, they said to Du, "Speak, and we will spare her."

Still he made no reply.

Then they whipped and beat her, shot and slashed

her, burned and branded her, till her whole body was streaming with blood and she was in agony.

"I know I am only a simple woman and not good enough for you," she cried. "But I have served you for more than ten years. Now devils have seized me and the pain is more than I can bear. I would not ask you to lower yourself to plead with them; but if you say just one word, my life will be spared. How can you be so heartless and grudge even one word?" Tears poured down her cheeks as she reproached and cursed him. Still Du paid no attention.

"Do you think I cannot kill her?" demanded the commander. Then he ordered the devils to fetch a chopper and chop off the woman's feet inch by inch. Du's wife screamed with pain, but still he paid no attention.

"This scoundrel is well versed in magic," said the commander. "We cannot let him live." And he ordered his guards to kill Du.

When Du had been killed, his spirit was haled before the king of hell.

"Is this the wizard of Yuntai Peak?" asked the king of hell. "Put him to torture."

Then melted copper was poured down his throat, he was beaten with iron rods, pounded with pestles, ground between millstones, thrown into a fiery pit, boiled in a cauldron and dashed against a forest of swords. But through all his sufferings he bore in mind what the priest had said, and let no groan escape his lips. When the jailers announced that all the tortures had been tried, the king said, "This is a scoundrel. He must not be allowed to be a man. Let him be reborn as a woman in the family of Wang Qin, the magistrate of Shanfu County in Songzhou."

Then Du was reborn as a woman. As a child she was delicate and often ill. Not for a single day was she free from painful medical treatment. Once she fell off the bed, and another time fell on to the stove. The pain was intense, but not a sound did she utter. She grew up into a beautiful girl but never spoke a word so that her family thought she had been born dumb. Her relatives insulted her in many ways, but she never retorted. A scholar from the same county, named Lu Gui, heard of this dumb girl's beauty and sent a match-maker to ask for her hand. When the family declined because she was dumb, Lu said, "She doesn't have to speak to make a good wife. And she will be a good example for women who talk too much." Then the family agreed, and Lu married Du with due ceremony. They came to love each other, and after they had been married several years Du gave birth to a son. Soon the child was two years old, and amazingly precocious.

Lu could not believe that his wife was really dumb. One day, holding the child in his arms, he spoke to Du, but the latter would not reply. Lu tried various ways to trick his wife into speaking, but still Du remained silent. Then Lu flew into a rage and said, "In ancient times the Minister Jia had a wife who despised him and would never smile; but after seeing what a good hunter he was she changed her mind. Now I am not as bad as Jia, and my literary talents are much superior to skill in hunting; yet you refuse to speak to me. What use is a son, when the husband is despised by his wife?"

Thereupon, seizing the child's feet he dashed his head against a stone. The little boy's skull was smashed, and blood spurted out several feet. Love for the child made Du forget the pledge and give an exclamation of horror.

While the exclamation was still on Du's lips, he found himself back on the seat in the hall, with the priest before him. It was dawn. Purple flames from the cauldron were shooting up through the roof to the sky, and fire was rising from all sides to burn the house to ashes.

"Look what you have done! You have spoilt my work, you silly fellow!" exclaimed the priest. Seizing him by the hair, he threw Du into a jar of water. Then the fire was extinguished.

"You succeeded in mastering joy, anger, sorrow, fear, hate and desire," said the priest. "Only love you could not overcome. If you had not cried out, my elixir would have been completed and you could have become immortal too. How hard it is to find a man who can attain godhead! Still I can brew my elixir again, while you remain a mortal and lead your own life on earth. Farewell!" Then he pointed out to Du his way back.

Du forced himself to look around. In the ruined cauldron was an iron rod as thick as a man's arm and several feet long. Taking off his outer garment, the priest began to cut this rod up with a knife.

After Du's return to the world, he felt ashamed to have failed to repay the old man's kindness and swore to himself that he would make good his failure. But when he went back to Yuntai Peak there was no one there. He had to return sadly home.

The White Monkey

Anonymous

IN the year 545, during the Liang dynasty, the emperor sent General Lin Qin on an expedition to the south. He went as far as Guilin, and wiped out the rebel forces of Li Shigu and Chen Che. At the same time his lieutenant Ouyang He fought his way as far as Changle, conquering all the cave-dwellers there and leading his army deep into difficult terrain.

Now Ouyang's wife had a white skin and was very beautiful and delicate.

"You should not have brought such a beautiful wife here," his men told him. "There is a god in these parts who carries off young women, especially good-looking ones. You had better guard her carefully."

Ouyang took fright. That night he set guards around the house, and hid his wife in a closely guarded inner chamber with a dozen maidservants on watch. During the night a high wind sprang up and the sky turned dark, but nothing untoward happened and shortly before dawn the exhausted guards dozed off. Suddenly, however, they were startled from their sleep to find that Ouyang's wife had disappeared. The door was still

---

This is a satire on the famous calligrapher Ouyang Xun who was reputed to look like a monkey.

locked, and no one knew how she had left. They started looking outside on the steep hillside, but a thick fog blotted out everything at one yard's distance, making it impossible to continue the search. Then dawn came, but still they could find no trace of her.

In great anger and grief Ouyang swore that he would not return alone. On pretext of sickness he stationed his troops there, and sent them out daily in all directions to search the valleys and heights for his wife. A month later, on a bush some thirty miles away, they found one of her embroidered shoes, soaked by rain but still recognizable. Overcome with grief, Ouyang intensified the search, taking thirty picked armed men with rations to scour the hills. After another ten days, they reached a place about seventy miles from their camp from where they could see a green, tree-clad mountain to the south which towered above the other hills. When they came to the foot of this mountain, they found it surrounded by a deep stream, which they had to build a little bridge to cross. Between the precipices and emerald bamboos they caught glimpses of coloured dresses and heard the sound of women talking and laughing. When they pulled themselves up the cliffs by vines and ropes, they found green trees planted in avenues with rare flowers between them, and a verdant meadow fresh and soft as a carpet. It was a quiet, secluded, unearthly retreat. There was a gate to the east, hewn in the rock, through which several dozen women in bright new dresses and shawls could be seen passing — singing and laughing as they went. When they saw the strangers, they stopped to stare. And when the men went up to them, the women asked what had brought them there.

After Ouyang had told them, the women looked at

each other and sighed. "Your wife has been here over a month," they said. "Just now she is ill in bed. You may go and see her." Passing through a wooden door in the stone gate, Ouyang saw three spacious enclosures where couches strewn with silk cushions had been placed by the walls. His wife was lying on a bed spread with matting and rugs, with rich food placed before her. At Ouyang's approach she turned and saw him, but signed to him to leave.

"Some of us have been here for ten years already," the other women told him, "while your wife has only just arrived. This is where the monster lives. He is a man-killer, a match for even a hundred warriors. You had better slip away before he comes back. If you will let us have forty gallons of potent wine, ten dogs for him to eat, and several dozen catties of hemp, we shall be able to kill him. Come at noon, not earlier, ten days from now." They urged him to leave quickly, and Ouyang did so.

He was back again on the appointed day bringing with him the strong liquor, hemp and dogs. "The monster is a great drinker," the women told him, "and likes to drink himself silly. When he is drunk he always wants to test his strength, and tells us to fasten his arms and legs with silken ropes as he lies on the couch. Then he frees himself with one leap. But once we twisted three ropes together, he couldn't break them. Now if we twist hemp inside the silk, we are sure he will never be able to snap it. His whole body is like iron, but he invariably protects those few inches under his navel; this must be his vulnerable spot." Then, pointing to a nearby precipice, they said, "That is where he stores his food. You can conceal yourselves there. Keep quiet and wait. Put the wine by the flowers and the dogs in the forest. If our plan works we shall call you."

Ouyang and his men did as they were told, and waited with bated breath. Late in the afternoon, something like a streamer of white silk flew down from the top of a distant hill straight into the cave, and in a little while a six-foot man with a fine beard came out. Dressed in white, with a stick in his hand, he was attended by the women. He gave a start at the sight of the dogs, then leaped at them, seized them and tore them limb from limb, eating greedily until he was sated. The women offered him drinks in jade cups, and together they joked and laughed gaily. After he had drunk several pints of wine, the women helped him in, and sounds of fun and merriment could be heard.

After a long time, the women came out to summon the men, who went in carrying their weapons. They saw a huge white monkey fastened by its four paws on the couch. At the sight of the men it recoiled and struggled in vain to release itself, and its furious eyes flickered like lightning. Ouyang and his men fell on it, only to find its body like iron or stone. But when they stabbed at its belly under the navel, their swords sank in and red blood spurted out. The white monkey gave a long sigh and said to Ouyang, "This must be the will of heaven — for otherwise you would not have been able to kill me. Your wife has conceived. Don't kill the child born to her, for he will grow up to serve a great monarch and your family will prosper." With these words he died.

They searched through his possessions, and found stores of precious things as well as an abundance of rare food on the tables. Every treasure known to man was there, including several gallons of rare scents and a pair of finely wrought swords. The thirty-odd women were all exquisite beauties, some of whom had been there for ten years. They said that when women grew old they were taken away, to what fate no one knew. The white monkey was the only one to enjoy these women, for he had no followers.

Every morning the monkey would wash and put on a hat, a white collar and a white silk dress, wearing the same in winter and summer alike. He had white fur several inches long. When he stayed at home he would read wooden tablets inscribed with hieroglyphics which no one else could decipher; and after he had finished reading he would put the tablets under a stone step. On a clear day he might practise sword play, and then the two swords would encircle him like flashes of lightning making a moon-like halo round him. He ate all manner of things, particularly nuts, and was also very partial to dogs, whose blood he loved to drink. At noon he would fly off to travel thousands of miles in half a day, coming back at night. Such was his custom.

Whenever something caught his fancy, he would not rest till it was his. At night he forwent sleep to gambol through all the beds, enjoying the women in turn. He could chatter away and discourse eloquently too, despite his simian form.

One early autumn day that year when leaves were beginning to fall, the white monkey had seemed in low spirits and said, "I have been accused by the mountain deities and condemned to death. But if I solicit the aid of other spirits, perhaps I shall escape." Just after the full moon, a fire sprang up under the stone step and burned his tablets. "I have lived a thousand years but never had a child," he said despondently. "Now this woman is with child, it means my death is near." Running his eyes over the women, he wept for a while. "This mountain is secluded and steep, and no man has set foot here before," he went on. "Looking down from the peaks I have seen packs of wolves with tigers and other wild beasts at the foot of the mountain, while not even a woodcutter has appeared on the heights. If it were not the will of heaven, how could men have come here?"

Ouyang then went back taking the jade, precious stones and beautiful treasures as well as all the women, some of whom were able to find their own homes. In a year's time Ouyang's wife gave birth to a son, and the child took after the monkey. Later Ouyang was condemned to death by Emperor Wu of the Chen dynasty. But an old friend of his, Jiang Zong, was partial to Ouyang's son on account of his outstanding intelligence and took him into his house. Thus the boy escaped death. He grew up to become a good writer and calligrapher and a well-known figure in his time.

目　　录